JumpStart

The Start Up Book *for* your Dream Business

For Max
and
All you Dreamers

*Imagination is the beginning of creation.
You imagine what you desire, you will
what you imagine and at last you create
what you will.*

GEORGE BERNARD SHAW
IRISH DRAMATIST AND SOCIALIST (1856 - 1950)

Jump Start

The Start Up Book *for* your Dream Business

SUE VIZARD

Panoma PRESS

JumpStart
The Start Up Book *for* your Dream Business

First published in 2014 by

Panoma Press Ltd
48 St Vincent Drive, St Albans, Herts, AL1 5SJ, UK
info@panomapress.com
www.panomapress.com

Book layout by Michael Inns
Artwork by Karen Gladwell

Printed on acid-free paper from managed forests.

ISBN 978-1-909623-34-7

The right of Susan Vizard to be identified as the author of this work has been asserted in accordance with sections 77 and 78 of the Copyright Designs and Patents Act 1988.

A CIP catalogue record for this book is available from the British Library.

All rights reserved. No part of this book may be reproduced in any material form (including photocopying or storing in any medium by electronic means and whether or not transiently or incidentally to some other use of this publication) without the written permission of the copyright holder except in accordance with the provisions of the Copyright, Design and Patents Act 1988. Applications for the Copyright holders written permission to reproduce any part of this publication should be addressed to the publishers.

This book is available online and in bookstores.

Copyright © 2013 Susan Vizard

Contents

Acknowledgements

Purpose

CHAPTER 1	*It's all going to be OK*	1
	Highlights	18
CHAPTER 2	*Let's go back to the beginning*	19
	Highlights	28
CHAPTER 3	*Unleash your superpowers*	29
	Highlights	46
CHAPTER 4	*Find your dream life and business life*	47
	Highlights	52
CHAPTER 5	*Clear your clutter*	53
	Highlights	70
CHAPTER 6	*Clarify your Vision*	71
	Highlights	86
CHAPTER 7	*Remember what you love about your business*	87
	Highlights	105
CHAPTER 8	*Learn to truly love your clients*	107
	Highlights	126

CHAPTER 9	*Bring your customers sunshine with your smile*	127
	Highlights	147
CHAPTER 10	*Broadcast your message and call in your clients (gone fishing)*	149
	Highlights	170
CHAPTER 11	*Don't be afraid to make mistakes*	171
	Highlights	182
	Finally	185
	References	187
	About the author	189
	Testimonials	191

Acknowledgements

Thank you to Mindy Gibbins-Klein and her Book Midwife team, especially Kate. You got my arse in gear and ensured this book happened.

It was great to be part of a team of fellow first-time authors for whom amazing things are also happening. Good luck to you all.

A huge thank you to the reviewers – Jane, Liz, Grace, Lisa, Elinor, Jonathan, Rose, Peter, Marie – for your time, patience and feedback. Your positive support and caring constructive feedback helped me more than you will ever know.

Thank you Judymay Murphy – you opened the door, showed me a new path, explained how to read the signposts and find the way to changing my life. You inspire me.

Without the love and support of Katharine Dever I would not have had the courage or wherewithal to tap into my superpowers in order to change my life. Thank you Kat. And thank you to my Alchemic Sisters.

I'd like to acknowledge Lucie Bradbury for Damsels in Success and their conferences at which I have heard inspiring, incredible speakers and met some amazing inspirational women. And thank you to extraordinary Dan too.

Thank you for the logos Max.

Thank you Bridget for generously loaning the right books at the right time.

Catriona, thank you for the work.

Kisses to Gill, Lori, Fiona, Lisa, Morag – for champagne, hugs, listening and cat care.

Purpose of this book

This book is written for people who have been in business for a little while and are feeling stuck, stalled, exhausted and demotivated. It is also for people who are thinking of going into business for themselves and want to avoid being stuck, stalled, exhausted and demotivated in the future.

The purpose of this book is to show you a light that isn't an oncoming train, to pick you up, brush you down, give you a virtual hug and get you going again, in a fun and friendly way. There are simple tools and techniques that will re-energise and motivate you and help you to feel positive about life and your business.

A jump-start in a book, if you will.

Read this book if you:

- ✓ *Are considering starting a business.*
- ✓ *Run your own business and are interested in some ideas and inspiration.*
- ✓ *Are about to start your business and wondering if you should get your business cards (don't yet).*

- ✓ *Have bought the business cards and don't know what to do next.*
- ✓ *Run your own business and are thinking of giving it up and going back to employment (hold fire).*
- ✓ *Have forgotten how to dream.*
- ✓ *Are taking life a little too seriously.*
- ✓ *Know you have something to give the world and it's just not happening, for whatever reason.*

How to work this book

This book will show you that you can have an extraordinary life and business, have fun loving what you do, attract your perfect clients and make money.

The book describes the ideal steps to take in order to start your business afresh. Within each chapter there are ideas, stories, examples and activities.

You could read this book in a couple of hours. However, in order for you to get most value from the book and really build your 'having fun making money' muscles, take your time. I recommend that you read a chapter a week, and invest a couple of hours in that week to work through the activities.

You will then have time to assess what you have learned before moving on to the next chapter.

The book has been written so that if you follow the chapters in order it can help you address issues and quandaries that occur in every business owner's life. Or you can just dip into a chapter dealing with a specific query that you have. Each chapter contains stories setting the context for the exercises. For the impatient readers among you the stories have been separated (in boxes) from the key messages and exercises, making it easier for you to get straight to the point. Some of us like the journey and the stories are for us.

At the end of each chapter there is a highlights page, to remind you of what was discussed in that chapter.

In order to make best use of this book you will need:

- ✓ *A couple of hours a week for 8-12 weeks – no rules, whatever suits you best.*
- ✓ *A new notebook and pens (multi-coloured are fun).*
- ✓ *An open mind and a willingness to work with/say hi to the kid inside you.*

The time you spend on this book is your investment in you. If you relish it, look forward to that time and have a little fun, you may find you learn the messages more effectively.

CHAPTER ONE
It's all going to be OK

**My background
– does any of this sound familiar?**

If you are sitting there, head in hands, asking yourself why you started this business, this book is for you. If you are tired, frustrated, putting on a brave face, worried about where the next client is going to come from whilst fretting about the clash with a meeting and school sports day, read on.

It wasn't like this when you were employed, was it? At least you knew where the money was going to come from at the end of the month. You may have been lucky enough to have health insurance, a company car, share issues, as well as a pretty decent salary – I was. You may have even loved your job; I did – well, I used to in a masochistic kind of way.

My story

My last 'proper' job was as a senior project manager in a huge call centre for a very successful TV company in Scotland. My background is call centres. I didn't know what I was going to do when I grew up (actually I have only just found out), so I took my mediocre academic qualifications and after working in a shop, moved to Essex with my boyfriend and joined BT. I was in Business to Business Sales and had a title: Commercial Officer. Oh it was wonderful, I even signed the Official Secrets Act and joined the Closed Union – yes, I am that old. It was a great job, flexi-time, well paid, fun. Well, fun until they wanted me to take part in a telesales trial. It was during the early days of proactively calling businesses and asking them to buy a phone system. I managed to avoid that for a while though by breaking my ankle. When I came back to work the trial had finished.

It's interesting how we put barriers up – health, emotional, physical – when we don't want to move out of our comfort zone – isn't it? It's a recurring theme in my life, perhaps in yours too? Have a think about that.

I transferred with BT back to my home town. Passed the promotion board and became 'management'. I joined the marketing team and became the Press and PR Officer for the BT District. That role really did stretch my comfort zone, but I enjoyed it and learned a great deal about what I love to do and am good at. BT's structure changed and I found myself back in a call centre managing a team – a very large team of people looking after BT's small to medium sized business customers. The role involved team meetings, appraisals, clashing personalities and asking people to do what they didn't want to do – namely sell. I understood that because I didn't want to sell either. So I got pregnant instead (avoidance), went on maternity leave and had my beautiful son. After seven months I returned to work to find that my team had grown and they were now a proper sales team with tough targets that I had to manage them to achieve. I was under horrible, horrible stress.

I worked very long hours, was away from home at least twice a month and was monitored on an hourly basis against call answering and sales performance team targets.

Forgive me for being self-indulgent but if you are who I think you are, parts of my story will resonate with you. And yes, this book is about you, and for you, but read on a bit longer because I would like you to know my background in order for you to feel you know me, a little, and the experiences we have in common.

Bit more background

I went back to work, still nursing my lovely big hungry boy who would never take a bottle. Perhaps deep down I didn't want him to, because I wanted to be needed by him as much as possible. Although in the first six months of his life I have never been as resentful of anyone as I was of him. Many working mothers among you will recognise a fellow control freak.

I expected myself to manage it all: my son, my team of 40-plus people, my managers, my husband, the house, the childcare and everything. I did really well for a while, but then I started to implode. My husband was working away during the week – and I had the additional pressures of being a week-time single mum. I didn't break, I just got desperately unhappy, blamed myself for not doing everything I thought I should, tried harder to succeed, failed and beat myself up some more. I know many of you are in that cycle of self-destruction.

I tried to get a transfer to Manchester, where my husband worked. The only role I was offered was within the same call centre structure. I realised that I could not take any more of that pain so I left BT, without taking release or retiring. I think they had to find a new form for me – in those days no one left BT voluntarily. In those days no one left anywhere voluntarily – hmmm, the good old days.

CHAPTER ONE - **It's all going to be OK**

Scotland background – getting there

My husband then got transferred to Scotland. Although I was unhappy with him too, we decided to stay together and try a new start, with me not working for a while. My son was three. I lasted three months before we agreed that being an 'at home mum' is even more difficult and stressful than working full-time. If you are a full-time housewife and mum, I salute you. I jumped ship and found a job at Sky working within the Marketing Call Centre Management team.

It was a great working environment. I loved the freedom, the flexibility, the pay, the flat management structure and I did well. I worked longer and longer hours, and my marriage collapsed through lack of attention. I got promoted, more pay, moved around and became an account manager, a project manager, team manager, senior project manager and stayed 10 years.

Until one day I was taken aside, given an offer I could not refuse, and I left.

Almost there, almost back at you, hang on.

Enforced freedom

And that's when I lost my sense of identity. I became a reflecting doormat. I tried to be what I thought other people wanted me to be. The long and the short of it was I couldn't even get that right. I know some of you will relate to that.

I worked in a deli. I loved the customers, and the food, but was disliked by the other people who worked in the deli. I was asked to leave.

I worked as an administrator for a private school, part-time for a year. They asked me to leave.

The money was pouring out. I worked as a freelance salesperson on behalf of a couple of clients. Turns out I was good at that, but then got caught up trying to solve all their problems, failing and leaving. I tried network marketing. I can sell, and I loved the products. It's great if you have staying power – as you can tell, I didn't. (By the way, if you are in network marketing this book is for you too.)

I lost my husband, my boyfriend, my youth (referring to my age, not a very young man), my hope and my Mercedes. I was in a huge amount of debt, juggling Peter credit card to pay Paul credit card. I still held my head high, tried to find clients, networked, told loads of people the current idea for my next big thing, but made no money and became desperate.

I hope that none of you are in that dark place, but if you are this book is for you too, with reassurance that it is all going to be OK.

> I changed my life by changing how I feel about my life. I went to a conference and heard a woman speak about money. She was gorgeous, sexy and individual, living a fun life meeting amazing people all around the world. She was fulfilling her powerful potential. She told me that I could do that too and I believed her.

Since then I have studied, worked with personal development books and coaches and business gurus. It soon became clear that I already had what I needed in order to live an extraordinary life, and so do you. All it takes is a few techniques and approaches, regularly practised, that after a while become part of your way of life. It's simple but definitely not easy.

I am not finished, life is a journey, but I am out of that place of pain and living a life I never dreamed I could have. If I can do it, anyone can.

In this book I share with you the tools and activities that help me with my life and business, in order to help you and save you a huge amount of pain, time and money.

Background story finished – over to you.

Right, let's get to work. Believe me when I say:

*You can have a great business,
loving what you do and the people you
do it for, have fun and make money.*

Yes you can – with help, with a bit of effort and with a willingness to let go of those rubbishy old beliefs about your limitations that you are carrying around with you.

If you are the reader I anticipate you are, you are seriously considering closing this book now, putting the kettle on and saying: "I knew it, she seemed like me but she is just another mad 'change the world, woo woo' person. Ugh! Must be time for *Loose Women* on the telly."

STOP! I am like you. That is why I am giving you this promise. If you read this book and do the exercises – properly now – and still feel hopeless, demotivated and have no ideas for you or your business, I will return to you the price of this book.

Why would I do that?

Because I believe that you can change your life, your business and your clients' experience for the better. This book will give you some tools, techniques and resources to help you do that in a fun way.

Here we go, into your first activity. This logo will alert you to the fact that it's time for you to have a go and get involved. There's also a bit of space at the end of the exercise for you to make notes, should you wish.

Could you have said this?

Over the years I have heard friends, colleagues and clients express the following sentiments and frustrations.

Go on, get your pen out and mark any of these statements that ring a bell for you:

- ☐ *I have a great business, great product, great service but I am frustrated because nobody seems to get it.*
- ☐ *I need to do more communicating.*
- ☐ *I need to do more networking, but I am too busy.*
- ☐ *I spend time and money networking but I am not meeting the right people, I haven't sold anyone anything networking.*
- ☐ *I don't know what to say when I meet people.*
- ☐ *Networking doesn't work.*
- ☐ *I don't see enough of my family.*
- ☐ *My husband (wife/son/daughter) is frustrated that I am not making enough money and wants me to stop and go back to employed life.*
- ☐ *I feel guilty all the time because I should/need to be more/better/different.*
- ☐ *There is so much I have to do, I just don't know what to focus on.*
- ☐ *I have run out of money.*
- ☐ *I feel lack of support.*
- ☐ *I'm stuck.*
- ☐ *I need to change something, but what?*

JumpStart *The* Start Up Book *for* your Dream Business

- ☐ *I want guidance, coaching, help but there's no time or money for that.*
- ☐ *I'll get coaching when I have £50,000 in the bank.*
- ☐ *I don't feel original.*
- ☐ *I don't like my customers.*
- ☐ *Why don't my team feel like I do about my business?*
- ☐ *I will get coaching when I have my team recruited/fired/sorted out.*
- ☐ *The business will work when I get myself/the team fired/recruited/sorted out.*
- ☐ *I just don't know the right people.*
- ☐ *I don't know how to sell.*
- ☐ *'So and so' has it easy.*
- ☐ *Perhaps I am in the wrong business/network marketing product/area/decade/life.*

_____

_____

_____

_____

_____

These statements and so many more like them have been said by at least one of my clients, friends or networking colleagues, and it is likely you have thought of a few of them too. What do these statements have in common? Yes, they are negative. They reflect that, in some way, you believe you are not 'good' enough to run your own business.

Well, that is **WRONG**. You are exactly **RIGHT**. Perfect. In fact, there is no one else that could be a better success at running your business than you.

- ✓ *Only you have your dreams.*
- ✓ *Only you have your qualifications.*
- ✓ *Only you have your life experience.*
- ✓ *No one else has your gifts and abilities.*
- ✓ *You can have the dream business, perfect clients, make money and have fun doing it.*

Changing how you feel about yourself will change how you see the outside world.

Therefore we will talk about what you believe in, your values and your self-belief.

People like to be with people they like or would like to be like. When you understand your values and beliefs you know more clearly who those people are for you and they become the people you would like to serve. And I do use 'serve' deliberately. If you are reading this book it is because you are looking for an answer, probably to one of the complaints listed above. Therefore you are fearful or frustrated. Do you know why? Because you have something which will help someone in some way and they are not buying it. You are frustrated in your need to serve.

And your self-belief? You will work on that throughout the book and throughout your life. In the meantime please accept that *you are in the right place of your life at the right time in your life, and everything is going to be all right*. Now you say it, aloud: "I am in the right place, at the right time and everything is going to be all right." Doesn't that feel better?

What else will you learn in this book?

- *You will learn how to have confidence in yourself, your gifts, business, clients and your way forward.*
- *You will pick up some tips as to how to maintain positive attitude and energy.*
- *You will have a spring in your step and a song in your heart.*
- *You will have fun.*
- *And make money doing all of the above.*

If I say so myself, that is not a bad package in a book.

But – oh and there is always a BUT!

The magic in this book will only work for you if you do the work in the book. You will be surprised at the changes that you can implement as a result.

Don't feel stress or pressure, there is no giant Monty Python big foot that is going to stamp on you if you don't do anything. I won't come after you with a big stick. Don't look so disappointed!

The magic is more powerful if you smile when you do the exercises. Dig out your coloured pens, scissors, sticky stars, have a favourite beverage of choice, or even a pal, and HAVE FUN. It helps the learning sink in. Think *Mary Poppins* and 'a spoonful of sugar'.

This chapter is called It's all going to be OK because you are exactly the right person, in the right place, at the right time in your life, to make your business work for you and everything is going to be OK.

One of my favourite sayings was 'With my luck, when my ship comes in, I'll be waiting at the airport.' Nah – not any more. I am always in the right place to receive my luck. Let's get you to the harbour too.

When You Wish Upon a Star

When you wish upon a star
Makes no difference who you are
Anything your heart desires
Will come to you

If your heart is in your dream
No request is too extreme
When you wish upon a star
As dreamers do.

Leigh Harline, Ned Washington,
'When you Wish Upon a Star',
Pinocchio, Walt Disney Studios

Only you have your dreams. And do you know the saddest thing? So many people are frightened to dream. They have no hope other than to get through the day and get to bed. Only a year or so ago that was me, it may be you today.

Wish Upon a Star

It is time for you to admit you have dreams and bring them to life!

If you could live any life, what would it look like? Who is living *your* life? Go and pinch a bunch of magazines from your hairdresser (that's what I did), put some music on (or Six Nations Rugby in my case – very inspirational), and start cutting, sticking and drawing in order to create a collage of your dreams.

Dream about what *you* want, where *you* want to go, who *you* want to be. Use anything – sound, materials – and influence all your senses. Hear the music, the sound of the engine, smell the salt of the sea, the Italian cooking, taste the kiss, the champagne, feel the sand, the cold mountain air and see the words, look at the photos of where you want to go. Don't limit yourself to the collage. Go and test drive the car. Go in the shop and try on the shoes, handbag or suit. Have a cup of tea in *the* hotel (I do that a lot). Have fun and play. Look at you now! You will be pleasantly surprised by how many of your dreams are relatively easy to achieve. And if they are not, start reaching for them now. Just dreaming a dream will change how you live your life. How are you going to compete in a biathlon before you are 50 if you don't learn to swim when you are 48? True story, met the lady today. How are you going to drive an Aston Martin if you can't drive or have lost your licence? Even if you start saving when you didn't before, that is a vital change in how you live your life. When you accept your dreams and you live your life on purpose, that's when you move towards your dreams and they move towards you. It's a universal law.

___

___

___

Real Life CV

I am not thinking school qualifications here. Every time you learn more you add to the portfolio of strengths that you can draw on to serve your clients. This exercise will also show you a little about your learning style too. How do you like to gather knowledge? How do you like to spend your time?

Think about the courses you have chosen to do over the last 10 years, the clubs you are a member of and what you do within them. Make a list of the evening classes you have started and maybe finished. Any management courses, football training, painting schools, dance classes, drama groups?

Write down what you did, what you learned, and approximate date.

List everything. Example:

Drama group, on stage. 2012/13. Learned focus and commitment; learning lines, taking part and attending rehearsals. Learned I love being on stage, confidence. Teamwork, supporting the cast.

Pat yourself on the back and be honest. Remember what you learned and enjoyed and also what you didn't enjoy, or weren't very good at.

This list is also going to help you in a later chapter when we look in more detail at your gifts and genius.

_____

_____

_____

_____

_____

_____

Playing with marbles

Our life experience carves and shapes us into who we are. It is true that what doesn't break us makes us stronger.

Have you visited Florence and been to see the statue of Michelangelo's David in The Accademia Gallery? As you walk through the hall where David stands, you pass huge chunks of marble on either side. Each of these beautiful marble unfinished pieces of art were on Michelangelo's to do list. The genius sculptor was unsure what shape he would carve from the marble he had sourced until he had chipped away at it a little and revealed the beautiful original colour, grain and shine of marble contained within. He would then use the gifts of that stone to create the most incredible, original work.

We are all like those chunks of marble. We are each already stunning, with different colours, crystals and textures within us. Even our flaws are needed to create our individual beauty. We work with life to create our life's work, and that is to carve ourselves into the most beautiful, precious, amazing creations that we can be, using the material we have.

Each of your life experiences has honed you, chipped away at you, perhaps even cracked you, in order to create an original being of amazing potential and beauty.

Play Marbles

**Ask *yourself* these questions –
write a story if you like:**

- ☐ *What is the most difficult life experience I have ever had?*
- ☐ *How did I react to it?*
- ☐ *What was the outcome?*
- ☐ *What did I learn?*

Repeat this process for any major life experience that is in your past, and note well what you learned.

_____

_____

_____

_____

Life is carving you in order to reveal the gifts within you. What you learn from life is your gift to help others.

Highlights

CHAPTER ONE
It's all going to be OK

- ✓ *This book is aimed at bright, frustrated business people who feel unheard and unappreciated.*
- ✓ *This book can change your life, your business and your clients' experience.*
- ✓ *Read a chapter a week, do the activities, and take time to assimilate your learning.*
- ✓ *You are exactly the right person, in the right place at the right time; only you have your dreams, qualifications and life experience.*
- ✓ *You have permission to dream, and dreaming will instantly change your life.*
- ✓ *It's all going to be great.*
- ✓ *Life is carving you in order to reveal the gifts within you.*
- ✓ *What you learn from life is your gift to help others.*

Activities:

- ☐ **Could you have said this? – page 9**
- ☐ **When you wish upon a star - page 14**
- ☐ **Your real life CV – page 15**
- ☐ **Play marbles – page 17**

CHAPTER TWO
Let's go back to the beginning

This chapter is all about the genesis of your business. It's an opportunity to discuss and understand what motivated you to start your own business, and whether working for yourself is what you really want to do.

People are driven by many different factors to become self-employed – to join the world of people who have an income that depends upon them being paid in response to a product or service that they offer. Self-employed people have broken away from the world of employment. They are no longer in thrall to the weekly or monthly payslip, and managers who are unlikely to be the main recipients of their products or service.

There is a world of difference between the two mindsets. A regularly paid employee is motivated by what motivates their direct line managers, and their responsibility is to serve them. An employee is not directly responsible for how their employer's company serves their customer base. An employee does not have full control and they do not have ultimate responsibility.

When you go into business for yourself, whether or not you receive income is totally dependent upon your skills, effort, staying power, understanding your customer thoroughly and constantly adapting to serve them what they value. Whether or not you employ people, *you* are in control of how much income you earn. The *response* of your income is in line with your *ability* – YOU ARE RESPONSIBLE. There is no protection from this fact.

You are running your own business if you, for example:

Are a consultant, coach, designer, are in network marketing, party plans, have a shop, warehouse, rent property, get income from gambling, play the stock markets, are an author, musician, actor, artist, speaker, read palms, freelance etc. Part-time or full-time.

When you control your income from your ability to get customers to value and pay for what you offer them, there is nowhere to hide. It is scary and stressful but it is also challenging and can be fun. You are also ahead of the game because it has been said that in the future we will all be self-employed in some form or another. No one has a job for life these days.

Having defined that you are a self-employed business owner, or that you want to be, let's go back to understanding what motivated you to adopt this role.

Where we are in life is a result of our choices and actions in our past. Our future is a result of our choices and actions in this present moment. You may have been thinking that you were 'forced into' being self-employed but please acknowledge there is always an employment opportunity,

CHAPTER TWO - **Let's go back to the beginning**

even if it's 'not what you're used to'. Rest assured that there will always be a vacant seat for you in a call centre.

Context story

I became self-employed by accident. I tried to hang on to being employed but, other than a half-hearted effort to get back on the corporate merry-go-round, I settled for part-time employed jobs.

I worked part-time in a deli, then part-time in a language school. Those experiences opened my eyes to the fact that many business owners did not want to sell. I met a supportive business coach who asked me to do some cold calling for him. I then did similar work for somebody else and realised that I could supply a service that people wanted and could charge for my work. The problem was I didn't want to make 'cold' calls. Then I had an inspired idea. Why not train other people to do it? I found a client who employed me to train his team, then work with his team, then make the calls, then employ people to make the calls, and for a while I was running his sales and marketing for him. After a while he had a team, created partly by me, to support his business; we parted ways.

Being forced to leave my well-paid job turns out to have been a beneficial experience, as has been the past few years of self-employment trial and error, although not all of it felt so good at the time. Without these painful times I would not have grown to appreciate you, dear reader: the difficulties you face, the uncertainties you overcome, the resilience, courage, initiative and determination that you have.

I chose self-employment because I could not face the pain of going back into full-time work in a pressurised job, giving them everything I had, or so I thought, and then being asked to leave, again, as if I was of no value. I did not proactively choose to work for myself. I did not plan it or really consider the implications of this choice. That is why I lost money flitting from one initiative to another. The financial rope I had to hang myself was very, very long and I played it out to the very last inch. I do not want anyone else to have to go to that scary 'cheque bouncing' place, created in large part by lack of forethought and understanding of what it really takes to be self-employed. Hence this particular chapter demanding that you question whether being self-employed is the right thing for you.

Did you jump or... were you pushed?

Please take some time to consider and write your answers to these questions. Be brutally honest with yourself.

Q1. Why did you decide to set up your own business?

Here are some suggestions to help you consider whether you were 'pushed out' of employment:

- ☐ *Lost your job.*
- ☐ *Couldn't find work.*
- ☐ *Illness.*
- ☐ *Change in family circumstances.*
- ☐ *Fear of going back into the same environment.*

CHAPTER TWO - **Let's go back to the beginning**

_____

_____

_____

Q2. If it was as a solution to a problem, what is/are the problem/s? What is it in your employed life you are trying to avoid?

_____

_____

_____

Q3. What are the motivations – the reasons you jumped into running your own business? What positive experiences are you intending to gain through being self-employed?

Some ideas:

- ☐ *Wanted more time with your family, your partner, for yourself.*
- ☐ *Wanted your efforts to be more directly rewarded.*
- ☐ *Wanted more money.*
- ☐ *You love what you do.*
- ☐ *Wanted to be independent of boss, manager.*

Take some time to write, muse on how and why you ended up in this place in your working life. Did you truly want to work for yourself or could you not face the alternative?

_____

_____

_____

Now we come to the purpose of this chapter: to get an honest understanding of a very important point.

Perhaps your business does not solve your problem.

Working for yourself is challenging. You have to promote yourself, speak up for yourself, stretch your comfort zone every day in order to tell people about your business and, more importantly, ask them for money.

If you want to be successful you cannot hide and neither can your doubts and insecurities.

Same stuff – different job?

List the fears and concerns that you have about your business.

- ☐ *I am worried because…*
- ☐ *What if…?*

Take some time and really think – is there anything that is not working? What situations cause you to feel nauseous or to wake up in the middle of the night?

_____

_____

_____

_____

_____

Now look at the list you prepared earlier about the reasons you started your business and have an honest think. If the original problem has not been solved by your new business, you will still be feeling stressed and in pain. Therefore the pain was not being caused by your employed job, or previous work. QED the pain is caused by something deeper and older and will need to be addressed in a different way.

This is a scary thought. But won't it feel better understanding why running your own business is maybe *not* solving all the problems that you were aiming to put behind you when you started working for yourself?

You may not have a boss anymore but what is your relationship with your clients? Do you sometimes resent them? Do you avoid talking to them directly? Perhaps the problem is lack of confidence in your skills and abilities. Or a lack of appreciation as to how being open to other people's feedback can help you develop.

Perhaps you wanted to start a business in order to spend more time with your family, but actually you are finding that your business is taking up even more time, or you feel conflicted because you are not doing enough. Clarifying how you want your business to fit into your life, in a more structured way, will solve that problem. We will be looking at that later in the book.

Perhaps you are reluctant to pick up the phone; maybe you don't think you are good at 'selling'. Many people think they are an awful salesperson but the skills you need to 'sell' are those that human beings use all the time. Yes – we will be talking about that too.

JumpStart *The* Start Up Book *for* your Dream Business

It's getting better every day

This is the last activity for this chapter, and possibly the most important. Please have a good honest think and answer this question.

Which motivations and life issues have I addressed through working for myself?

_____

_____

_____

_____

Yes, some of your key concerns **will** have been solved. Do you now have more time, more independence, more control? Are you less stressed? Happier? Do you have more flexibility in work location? Can you walk to your office? Claim expenses against tax? Spend more time with the kids?

Clarify in your mind which problems have been solved by this independent life, note the positive solutions.

WRITE DOWN ALL THE GOOD STUFF. You are going to need it later.

_____

_____

_____

_____

Now you have a much clearer idea of how you came to be where you are. You also understand better the motivations and concerns that you were hoping to address through becoming self-employed, and the ones that are still impacting your life and your business.

That's good work – well done. Treat yourself!

Change

Humans don't like change. We will do almost everything we can to avoid it. This is strange behaviour because, like death and taxes, change is inevitable and unavoidable.

There are two drivers for change in our lives.

The first, and sadly the most common driver for most of us, is pain. Only when we are forced to admit that the pain of staying in our current situation is unbearable and anything else will be better, will we change.

The second driver for change, the positive one, is having a vision for how we want our lives to be and choosing to implement changes in order to follow the path towards that vision.

Whatever reasons drove you to change in the past, you now, through these activities, have a clearer idea of the issues you were trying to address and an idea of any outstanding concerns.

You may be wondering whether you are right for a self-employed life. Read on, there will be some useful exercises helping you make that decision.

But if you want an answer now? Ask yourself "Am I having any fun?" Do you smile at the thought of your business and the gifts it brings to your clients?

If yes – fantastic! If no – that's also fantastic, you have learned something useful.

Highlights

CHAPTER TWO
Let's go back to the beginning

- ✓ *People become self-employed for various reasons – understand yours.*
- ✓ *Understanding whether your motivation to work for yourself solves your life problems.*
- ✓ *Perhaps your business does not solve your problem – working for yourself brings many different challenges.*
- ✓ *Change, like death and taxes, is inevitable. Be in control.*

Activities:

- ☐ **Did you jump or were you pushed - page 22**
- ☐ **Same stuff, different job - page 24**
- ☐ **And it's getting better - page 26**

CHAPTER THREE
Unleash your superpowers

If that doesn't appeal, then imagine yourself twirling very fast and, as you gather speed, all the rubbish and baggage that you are carrying comes flying off, revealing you in your gorgeous costume and gold belt. Tiara too, if you wish. Wonder Woman!

George Bernard Shaw said: *Life is not about finding yourself. Life is about creating yourself.*

In this chapter we will look at some of the ways in which we have gathered and held on to negative restrictive thoughts and patterns throughout our lives, and consider how these messages have limited us and prevented us from revealing our true selves.

We will also look at how, when you understand these messages and have recognised them for what they are and let them go, you will begin to feel different about yourself, about life, and about what you can bring to your business.

There are also a couple of fun activities for you to do in order to unleash those superpowers.

By the end of this chapter my intention is that you feel amazing, as if you could leap tall buildings in a single bound, or even make a couple of phone calls to potential clients. Hmm, what colour should your cloak be?

This Be the Verse
By Philip Larkin

They f**k you up, your mum and dad.
They may not mean to, but they do.
They fill you with the faults they had
And add some extra, just for you.

But they were f**ked up in their turn
By fools in old-style hats and coats,
Who half the time were soppy-stern
And half at one another's throats.

Man hands on misery to man.
It deepens like a coastal shelf.
Get out as early as you can,
And don't have any kids yourself.

You are believing messages about who you are that are *not* true.

Babies are born with gifts and personalities. Every one of us is a precious special rough diamond, given to our parents to guard, protect and guide through childhood before releasing us into adulthood, with life's cuts and polish enhancing our beauty.

Babies are also amazing learning machines. We use all of our senses to understand how to survive and be loved, especially from birth to four years old when being loved is the only way we *can* guarantee survival. We don't have judgement based on previous experience to understand whether the way we are being cared for is appropriate or not. We accept our carers as they are, love them, and behave in such a way as to get them to love us. Therefore we either copy their behaviours, or we behave in the way we have been told we *should*, in order to be loved.

And this is where the challenge lies, ah you've guessed it, nobody's perfect! (Lucky nobody. Wasn't that the nickname for an Australian rugby player, John Eales?) I digress.

So the recipe for the mixed-up person you are today, with all your hang-ups and fears is:

1. *Take one amazing baby with its own individual personality and gifts.*
2. *Pass it through the first few years of life being yelled at, played with, fed, cuddled, bashed, influenced by television and books, but most of all by the non-stop movie show that is the way their family interacts with them and each other.*
3. *And the result is YOU, a wonderful superhuman in the making.*

Nothing you didn't know already, right? But now is the time to understand that the messages you heard about who you are, how you are permitted to behave, and the limits on your talents and potential – those messages about you that soaked into your brain, body and heart as truth – are

FALSE. They do not belong to you. They are your parents', family's, friends' beliefs about *their* lives and experiences, not yours. In order to survive and be loved as a child you soaked them in and made them your own. It's time to examine those messages, really look at them, and let many of those beliefs go.

I can hear you yelling at me: "But my dad told me I was beautiful" and "My mum told me I could do anything if I worked hard enough." Yes, many of the things our parents said to us were positive. Remember, however, that babies learn with *all* of their senses. Watching how people behaved will have influenced us as strongly, if not more so, than words.

You are old enough, strong enough, experienced enough to look at those books of messages on your brain shelf, take them down, dust them off and assess whether or not you are going to believe and accept them as *your* beliefs and values. If not then it is time to BURN them, completely eradicate them from your brain. Perhaps it's a cleaner metaphor to see those messages as old computer code. It is at the base of all your thoughts and behaviours. This code, which you didn't write, has programmed your life up to now. How unnerving is that? How can you be truly yourself when you are basing everything you do on other people's screwed-up hang-ups!? It's a wonder we are not all shivering schizophrenics!

We all hear other people's negative voices in our heads – you're not the only one. It's time to shut those voices up and overwrite that code. Then you will be in the minority of people who are making their *own* choices.

It is possible to understand these messages, who said them to you and perhaps consider why they were said. With understanding comes acknowledgement enabling you to forgive yourself and hopefully forgive others too.

Start building your own positive beliefs about yourself and then, Wonder Woman, the only limits you have to what you can achieve are the limits that you set yourself. How terrifyingly exciting is that?

Change will come as you change

As you tune into your positive messages about yourself, you will feel and react differently to the world around you. You will feel energised, enthusiastic, as if you have fallen in love, which you have – with you!

Nothing worth gaining is easy and life change is not immediate, it's gradual.

Many of us join a health club to get fit, or join a diet group to lose weight. However, unless we change how we talk to ourselves and how we feel about ourselves, the change to our fitness or weight will not last long term. If you commit 100% to being fit then something changes inside. There is a sense of wellness, a growing self-respect because you are treating yourself and your body with love. You begin to appreciate what a wonderful gift it is to feel good and you value that good feeling. And things that do not tune in with feeling good you gradually let go because you no longer think about them.

This course for your business life is the same. You are learning new approaches and techniques. They will seem strange to apply at first, and then, as you train and practise, they will become part of you. As you consciously apply new positive ways of doing things, after a while there'll be no space for the old ways.

There is a health warning though. Our resistance to change is HUGE and it is tricky to overcome. How many times have I started a diet with a huge binge – argh? How often have I said to myself: "Oh, I am going to work hard tomorrow so I will take a day off today"? Countless. The harder we see change to implement, the less likely it is that we will ever do it.

So my advice to you, and me, is little and often. Think *Shawshank Redemption.* Make a tiny chip away at the wall of change every day until the hole is big enough to escape through.

That is a great film to watch by the way. Andy Dufresne (the main character played by Tim Robbins) helps, supports and contributes inside the prison while he plans his escape. It's as if the knowledge that he is doing something every day to get *out* of prison, i.e. he had control and options, meant that he felt more positive about the people around him.

Although we all have our own dreams there is nothing to stop us helping others to achieve their dreams along the way. As we learn to love and respect ourselves, our ability to love and respect others increases too.

"Yeah, yeah, that's all very well but Dufresne, you, 'they' have it easy. I don't know how to chip away at my wall and anyway life is OK as it is, I don't need to change." Is there a little voice inside you that is saying that?

Eliminate the negative

It's time to listen to the negative voices inside your head and understand what they are saying, in order to lance the boil and release the poison of those messages.

Go into a very safe environment, somewhere where you are alone and no one can hear you scream. Keep a big box of tissues handy and write down the answers to these questions:

- ☐ *My life isn't going right because...?*
- ☐ *I am unhappy because...?*
- ☐ *It will be better when...? happens*
- ☐ *When I have...? then I can do...?*
- ☐ *When I have...? then I will be...?*
- ☐ *I can't do ...? because I am not...?*
- ☐ *I can't do...? because I don't have...?*
- ☐ *My business will be better when...?*
- ☐ *I will never succeed because I am...?*
- ☐ *I am no good because...?*

Take a good couple of hours and write all the rubbish down. All the beliefs you have about yourself. Really purge yourself, remember the hurt you felt when someone said something negative about you and write it down too. Dive deeply into a big pool of hurt and self-pity.

This exercise will cause you to feel pain and exhaustion. So as soon as possible afterwards go for a walk outside. Breathe and let it all go. Just let the fresh air, the birds, trees, light, fill the void left by those harsh words you have said about yourself. Forget what you have written and let nature wash it away.

When you are ready, perhaps after a couple of days, come back to this list of old beliefs. This list is going to be reality checked.

Truth or dare

The objective of this task is to slay, forever, the beastly beliefs that you have downloaded. To discredit their veracity so thoroughly that you will never believe them again.

You are going to ask two questions of each of the negative statements that you wrote in the previous exercise.

1. *Is that statement true all of the time?*
2. *Is that statement true some of the time?*

If the statement is true only some of the time then it means that sometimes it is untrue. Therefore it is not a true statement.

Those statements you have written are NOT fact, NOT truth. They are your old beliefs. Assumptions that you can challenge, should you choose to. This exercise is all about debunking these beliefs, seeing behind the curtain and showing them for the frauds they are.

Example statement: "I can't sell"

Why don't we challenge this frequently heard statement "I can't sell", which you may have written (I have certainly heard a lot of people say it), as an example.

The first question to ask of your statement is: "Is the statement 'I can't sell' true all of the time?" Well is it? Let's answer that question and look for evidence of when you have 'sold'.

Has anyone ever paid you for a product or service that you have provided? Yes, they will have done or you would not be running your own business.

Oh, you want more proof, you still don't think you can sell? Were you ever employed? If so, you used your selling skills to get that job, you used selling skills to keep that job. More? If you have children, whenever you persuade them to go to bed when they don't want to, those are selling skills.

You may do it through persuasion, flattery, bribery or reason but you are meeting their need for sleep, overcoming their objections and getting a result: them in bed and peace for you! That is selling. Therefore you have sold and the "I can't sell" statement is not true all of the time.

Please accept that the example statement "I can't sell" is unlikely to be true for any of us 100% of the time. In fact very few statements are true 100% of the time. Still not convinced? OK, let's allocate "I can't sell" a percentage for you. Let's say you can't

> sell for 95% of the time. Stop screaming at me – this is for your own good! Yes, this means that for a small percentage of time you can sell. Repeat after me: "This means that I can sell 5% of the time." Voila!
>
> There was probably an easier way to explain this exercise.

OK, now it's your turn.

Go through each and every one of your negative, destructive statements and test them, by asking if the statement is 100% true, or true some of the time. Write by the side of the statement the reasons why it is not 100% true and what you perceive the percentage to be. Most importantly, feel the relief of letting that absolute belief go. Feel the weight of that crippling burden lift from your shoulders. Feel yourself taking control and feeling freer. Feel yourself becoming more you.

_____

_____

_____

_____

Are your beliefs always true? NO.

Are they sometimes false? YES – which means that the negative code you have been working with is rubbish – false – untrue.

Oops there goes another rubber tree plant

You now have a list of negative statements where you will have reluctantly noted down by the side to what extent it is untrue.

You are now going to build yourself a to do list, based on emphasising what you *can* do with what you have and who you are. Rewriting that brain code so that you believe in YES.

Let's continue to use the sham 'I can't sell' as an example. On another piece of paper write on the top 'I can sell a little bit', whatever the percentage is, and then write the skills that you used in order to sell, a little bit. Or picture in your head when you sold something and remember how you did it; what happened, what did it sound and feel like? Then think about how you can use one or more of those skills in order to sell again, and start applying that skill with the objective of selling. Build new code, positive examples of when you did sell and how you CAN sell AGAIN.

And there will be the 'I don't have enough money' statement. Is that 100% true? Will that stay 100% true? No. Think about how you are spending your money at the moment. Are you buying food? Paying bills? Could you save some money each week? Yes you could. At some point in the future, if you save, earn, change your priorities, you will have enough money. So that statement is not 100% true. It's 99% true and so therefore it is false. Prove it so. Write down 'I have enough money, how could I have more?' List ideas and ways in which you can make a little more money each week.

_____

_____

_____

_____

Let's review where we are and check that you are still with me.

Firstly we looked at the fact that the beliefs which guide the behaviour of adult human beings are as a result of the blend of personality they were born with and the messages they derived from their closest carers when they were children.

You worked through a process which showed you some of the negative self-beliefs that have influenced your adult life to date. And, if the process worked, you will have recognised that many of these beliefs are false assumptions, and therefore of no value to you, and can be ditched unceremoniously as soon as possible ONCE you have understood and started to act in ways that will support new positive self-beliefs: 'I can sell,' 'People do like me,' 'I have enough money.' These statements are all potentially TRUE because they cannot be proved to be false. QED.

Then we looked at the fact that once we release some of the negative beliefs and start believing and trusting in our gifts and the good stuff, we feel better, healthier and happier. We are firmly on the path to becoming superhuman!

There you are, shivering in the cold having let go of many layers of your negative beliefs. You'll get chilly if you don't get your costume on quickly. Replacing them with positive beliefs will take a little time, but the ant didn't knock down the rubber tree plant in one go, and the guy didn't escape from Shawshank prison in one day either. You practise a little every day. And when you think a negative thought like 'I can't do this', you test out that statement with 'Is that thought going to be 100% true for always?' That's unlikely, very unlikely, and so therefore false.

So, if it's something you want to do, start thinking about ways you **can** do it.

Yes you are a Wonder Woman/Man in the making. Wouldn't it be useful now to understand your superpowers? And you have them, you really, really do.

Faster than a speeding bullet, can leap tall buildings in a single bound. Is it a bird? Is it a plane?

Each of us is born with talents and gifts that make us unique and wonderful. I believe that our gifts are honed and developed by the toughest times in our lives. When you understand what your gifts are and you begin to live in a way whereby those gifts are being used to their fullest extent, that's when dreams come true. What are your amazing superpowers?

Until a few months ago, and the rest of my life before that, I had no idea that I had gifts let alone superpowers. I believed that I was not at all special or different. Perhaps you believe the same thing? But I have listened to and worked with some amazing people over the last couple of years who have shown me how to acknowledge and accept my gifts. It has been a really powerful and emotional revelation, and not a little scary.

Our deepest fear is not that we are inadequate. Our deepest fear is that we are powerful beyond measure. It is our light, not our darkness that most frightens us.

- MARIANNE WILLIAMSON

Many of us are so fearful of not conforming, of being different from our friends and family, that we have never been honest about what we really want to *do* and who we want to be. We suppressed our gifts, like Superman tried to do as the boy Clark Kent. We are rarely shown that our power lies in our difference, not in our similarity.

Who did you pretend to be as a child? What did you imagine you were doing? Gay Hendricks (author of *The Big Leap*) tells a story about how, aged six or seven, he would set up a little desk in the corner of the living room and invite people to go to him with problems and he would listen to them. Apparently he lived in a small hick town in the States and people had never even heard of psychiatrists or therapists but that's what he felt he needed to do.

Your gifts are wired into your being and you display them from an early age, you can't help yourself.

CHAPTER THREE - Unleash your superpowers

Background context

My son is intelligent and talented. He is currently at university studying Computer Arts. He is good at maths, can draw, and did very well at school designing and creating with computer software. You would think that this is the ideal course for him and, to a certain extent, it is. He will become skilled and confident at invaluable computer technical wizardry. But he is not using his superpowers.

My son's gifts are his perception, analysis and recognition, which he uses with wisdom, love and loyalty. I know that he will be able to work at a job with his Computer Arts skills, but he will not be inspired and fulfilled unless his gifts are exploited and tested to their fullest.

If you want to know what your gifts are, ask your mum or your dad.

Perhaps you loved sports. But how did you love them? For example, were you passionate and self- motivated? Would you cycle down to the sports ground and be first there? Or, like a neighbour's son, would you carry your golf clubs half a mile uphill to the course, just to hit a few balls whenever you could? Your hobbies tell you a lot about your gifts too.

What did you want to be when you grew up? You may have wanted to be a nurse, teacher, professional footballer. OK – but why? And what kind of nurse, how do you nurse?

> I always wanted to be a jet pilot. As I think about it now, I wanted to be alone. When I look back I was often alone. Up trees, walking to school, hiding away in my room in a dream world. And yet everyone thinks I am an extrovert. I thought I was. I know now that, by nature, I am an introvert dreamer who was frightened of dreaming for many years.

Did you draw, paint, build, talk, sing, act, create, copy, write, run, dance, give, cook, show off?

What can you do for hours and hours without getting restless? There may be several different things. Think about what you're doing when you don't notice time passing.

Your gift will possibly not be the action that you do, but the way in which you do it. What have your friends, colleagues, bosses complimented you on? One of my superpowers is enthusiasm. Not everyone has it!

Phonebox or Batmobile?

Get a big piece of paper and some coloured pens or, if you prefer, record yourself speaking, or draw images, however your brain likes to explore and download information. And answer this question:

WHAT DO I *LOVE* TO DO?

Start to write down some words:

> ☐ *I love...*
> *... being outside, inside, movement, stillness, focus, planning, teamwork, leading.*

Other questions to consider are:

- *What jobs did you apply for? What type of work appeals?*
- *Think back on your achievements – what has really given you a huge sense of satisfaction? What skills did you use in order to achieve that? e.g. persistence, focus, supportiveness, enthusiasm.*

Take time to think about it, day dream – the words will come to you.

_____

_____

_____

Finding your gifts and talents, uncovering new ones, beginning to use your gifts effectively, living and working while using your superpowers – all this will increase your passion to seek opportunities to use and stretch your powers further.

This chapter is all about encouraging your awareness of old beliefs, testing their veracity and letting go of the ones that are not true. When you have done this work you can begin to find and work with your innate gifts, your superpowers. This work will continue for the rest of your life. Your life becomes a journey of discovery of how best to use your gifts for the benefit of yourself and others.

There are many resources and people with positive information to share; some are listed at the end of the book.

JumpStart The Start Up Book *for* your Dream Business

Highlights

CHAPTER THREE

Unleash your superpowers

✓ *You believe messages you have received throughout your life about who you are that are not true.*

✓ *When you discover your true amazing self, without these false beliefs, you will feel transformed.*

✓ *Life is a journey of discovery of your superpowers.*

✓ *Steps to unleashing the power within you:*

- ☐ *Understand the past beliefs*
- ☐ *Test their validity*
- ☐ *Create new positive beliefs*

Activities:

- ☐ **Eliminate the negative - page 35**
- ☐ **Truth or dare - page 36**
- ☐ **Oops there goes another rubber tree plant - page 39**
- ☐ **Phonebox or Batmobile? - page 44**

CHAPTER FOUR

Find your dream life and business life

(how are you going to have a dream come true?)

When you have a dream – everything becomes simpler

Please note I didn't say life becomes easier; no, it's still challenging, but it becomes simpler. Why? Because you begin to bring all the strands of your life together in order to make your dream come true. And if there are areas of your life that do not move you closer to your dream then you understand why you need to let them go.

I have visited the thesaurus. The dreaming I want you to take a bit of time to do is a process of inventing, creating, devising, desiring, fantasising. Become visionary and enjoy!

Perhaps you don't have a dream of how you want your life to be, and if your life to date has been difficult, or you felt you weren't worthy enough to dream, it's understandable that dreaming is difficult for you. However, as we have discovered already, you did start your business (or are thinking about a business), and *everyone* who starts their own business has a dream. No exception. Even if that dream is well submerged under fear, it is there. You believe that you can create a better working environment for yourself than an employer can and that is a dream, a vision. You visualise something different from what you have and want to have a go and make it real. That is creation and all creators are dreamers.

Lights, Camera, Action!

We are now going to turn your Vision Board and the dream images and ideas in your head into a virtual movie with Panavision, Smell-O-Vision, feelavision, and tastavision.

To make this really effective and fun it would be good to do this exercise with a friend.

You are going to make a recording so that you can play it back whenever you wish. If you are working with a friend ask them to record it for you and ask you the questions to keep you on track.

There are some guidelines to understand before you go dreaming. You are going to dream an ideal day in your life. You are to create a vision of the work you would do, how you would do it, who for, and where, AS IF YOU DID NOT NEED THE MONEY. I also want you to accept a few things about your life before you start to dream so that you do not concern yourself with them as they are not relevant for this dream.

DREAM RULES:

- *You are the person you always dreamed you would be. You are the size and shape you want to be, you have the love of your life by your side supporting you, and you have all the money you need to do whatever you want to do.*

- *You have been on holiday for as long as you needed and you are now ready to work. It is this first working day that you are going to visualise. By 'working' I mean that you create something: a product or experience.*

- *Do not limit yourself. You can be and do ANYTHING. You are superhuman and amazing. This is a dream. Let the cameras roll, no cutting or editing.*

- *Be as specific as possible. You need to remember this dream like you remember the best day in your life.*

Right, let's begin. Sit or lie down, close your eyes and start talking. Start recording. Imagine yourself waking up. Where are you? What does your room look like? Your love is beside you, all is well, you can leave them and start your day. What do you do? How do you want to start your day?

Think about what you eat, if you exercise, how? Imagine your work, your business. What do you do? Where do you go? Are you at home or in an office? Do you have a studio? A stage? Are you alone or with other people? Imagine it: where do you go, what happens next? Are you outside? Inside? Feel the air on your face, hear the people beside you. Who are they? What are they doing? How are you contributing to your life or their lives? What are you doing? How are you doing it?

Record your dream. Talk for as long as you feel you want to, half an hour is likely to be more than enough time. Then stop the recording.

While you still remember your dream write things down: ideas, new thoughts, things that surprised you. Hold on to the images in your mind.

Start to clarify this dream life and business of yours. Your next action is to write down the answers – the dream answers, remember – to the What, Where, When, How, Who questions.

What are you doing? Where are you? When during your day/week do you work? How long for? How do you work? Are you working with your hands, physical work? Or are you speaking, writing? Are you on a PC or with a pen? Do you have an office, do you visit people? Do you work with materials, food, words, music? What are you wearing? How do you look? Who are your clients? Do you have a team? What do they do? Who are the people you want to work with? Can you think of anyone? Write down their names.

If your dream is different from what you are currently doing, that is absolutely great. In fact if any item is different from your current life that is good too. It means that you have accessed the creative part of your brain, the part that doesn't hear the negative voices, but does tune into your gifts. You are in the right place at the right time and on your way.

Write it down, scope it, picture it, listen to your recording regularly, this will be the basis for your business plan, honestly it will.

Remember your life is about creating success, love and abundance. Creating something with your gifts is how you do it. Idleness is not an option, not if you wish to feel fulfilled. But if you are working with your superpowers then work does not feel like work, it feels like a way of life.

OK – time to bring yourself back to reality. Did you enjoy that? Good work, well done.

Ooh, don't forget to allow your friend to go through the same process! Maybe at a different time so they are not influenced too much by your dream.

___

___

___

___

Dreaming, like everything, takes practice. But every so often take half an hour to dream actively.

You may have dreamt something very different from what you do – for example, becoming a pop star or a jet pilot. Over the next couple of chapters we are going to question your dreams and begin to see what it is about becoming the next Beyoncé, or flying alone and brave in the skies, that attracts you. It could be that when you scope and understand your dream and it becomes a Business Vision and Plan that you may have to consider just how your power becomes a way to give to others and therefore a way to earn payment.

JumpStart *The* Start Up Book *for* your Dream Business

Highlights

CHAPTER FOUR
Find your dream life

Happy talk, keep talkin' happy talk,
Talk about things you'd like to do.
You got to have a dream,
If you don't have a dream
How you gonna have a dream come true?

If you don't talk happy,
And you never have dream,
Then you'll never have a dream come true!

- RODGERS AND HAMMERSTEIN:

SOUTH PACIFIC, 1949

✓ *When you have a dream, life becomes simpler.*
✓ *Dreaming takes practice.*
✓ *Effective dreams involve all your senses.*

Activities:

☐ **Lights, Camera, Action**
   – page 48

CHAPTER FIVE
Clear your clutter

Since my house burned down I now own
a better view of the rising moon.

MAZUTO MASAHIDE 1657 - 1723

Have a quick look at what you have tackled so far in this jump-start to your business life. I hope you are standing tall knowing that everything is going to be just right and that you are in the right place.

So far you have considered why it was that you started your business; whether it was because you positively wanted a better life for yourself, or more negatively because you could not bear to stay in the job you were in.

You have also thought a little about whether your business will solve your concerns and issues, or if it has just magnified them.

If you are feeling frustrated you now have a clearer understanding as to where that frustration lies. You have visualised your dream business life, what that looks like and how it feels.

You have also looked at who you are, had a think about your talents and skills and begun to discover your true superpowers.

In the 'Find your dream life and business life' chapter you began to review how you would like your future to be. This next part of the book is all about preparing yourself to head towards that dream.

> *We are like sailors who must rebuild their ship on the open sea, never able to dismantle it in dry-dock and to reconstruct it there out of the best materials.*
>
> **NEURATH (1932/3)**

Transformation of any kind requires endings and clearance.

Moving house story

This time last year I was living in a beautiful big four-bedroomed house with a double garage, long drive, separate utility room, dining room, ensuite bathroom etc.

I realise that it doesn't matter what the house looked like, it was a symbol of my status and my place. Successful career woman, good mother, excellent housekeeper, good neighbour, middle-class, appropriate, fitted in with my neighbours, was not a bother.

I was hanging on to it even though I was single, my son had started university and I had huge debts that were just getting worse. I was lonely, frightened and overwhelmed by all the stuff I carried in my life. My cluttered house symbolised my life. Too big, filled with furniture, old photos, decorations, tools, files and notebooks that were the detritus of my past and constantly reminded me of the roles I used to have, but no longer fulfilled. Those roles of wife, partner, highly paid employee, mother to a school-aged child, party girl and label purchaser. I knew how to acquire, just didn't know how to let go. And it was weighing me down, blocking my view. I could not see the future, had no hope, no dreams, could not see past all the stuff that reminded me, every day, of all the things I was not any more. I didn't know how to see all the things I could be.

A neighbour lent me a book about clearing clutter. Sadly that book in itself was not enough to initiate the change.

The change came because I was sinking into debt. I was capital rich and income poor. The pain became unendurable and moving was the only solution (remember what initiates change?). Oh, I resisted it big style. In fact I was so desperate to hang on to the status of living where I lived, I only moved a few hundred yards. Initially this new house was a compromise, but now it is a big win. But the biggest win was experiencing the change and declutter process.

Once you start this process of 'letting go' it becomes a crucial part of moving on in your life. You cannot have change without ending something. The universe abhors a vacuum.

And you are off again, I can hear you: "Well, bully for you, but how is this relevant to me and my business?" The process is extremely relevant, let me show you why.

What is clutter?

Clutter is the stuff that prevents you from seeing clearly. It is the barrier to your progress. It is the blockage in your path, the stuff that protects you from change. Until you recognise and remove the clutter from your life and business you will not be able to change your business for the better.

The negative beliefs we hold about our ability are also clutter. Think how much lighter you feel now you have let some of that mental junk go.

Clutter is not necessarily stuff, it can be old habits, things you do to procrastinate. I just had an article of my clutter jump on to my lap and demand attention, the beautiful distraction which is my cat.

For some reason we allow ourselves to get into a routine of things we need to do before we work. I make a coffee, then I listen to something, then I do something else, phone my mum, then I top up my coffee. Often it's an hour before I start to work and I have eaten into the time allocated to writing.

Clutter can be promises and commitments which are no longer relevant to your business, or to your life, and add no value to anyone.

Clutter can be a reflection of how we think and what we prioritise.

What does your working area look like?

Everything from the smallest bug to a sheet of A4 paper is a bundle of atoms being held together by energy. Everything has a vibration. Items that are scattered around you, but not of use, will vibrate anyway and drain your energy.

Clutter and procrastination do go hand in hand. Have a look at the people you spend time with, the meetings you go along to. Do you surround yourself with people who are positive? People who you would enjoy working with? Are your networking events supportive of your business aspirations? Negative people and events impact on your energy too; they are a form of clutter.

Why clear your clutter?

The process of regularly looking at what is important, and letting go of what is not, is vital for change. Think of snakes shedding skin and remember we shed skin too. It's natural to clear our clutter! Reviewing your priorities and focusing on what you really need to do will help you let go of what is not necessary. Life is a journey, not a destination.

If you want a golden rule that will fit everybody, this is it: Have nothing in your houses that you do not know to be useful, or believe to be beautiful.

WILLIAM MORRIS IN 1880

It is time to lighten your load to make space for new ideas.

How?

Let's think about physical items first.

Consider my house move as an example.

I moved into a smaller space from a larger space, a real quart into a pint pot. I lost a bedroom, dressing room, dining room, garage and an awful lot of wardrobe space.

I thought about the bare essentials: beds, bedroom furniture, sofas, table, chairs. My son could now move to a double bed. He wanted to keep his cabin bed, but sleep in the double bed. Nope – the cabin bed had to go, thank you eBay. Difficult decisions for everyone. Antique dining table and chairs went to the auction rooms. Piano on to Gumtree. Bedroom furniture I had no room for: eBay. Study shelves went into the single garage to allow storage. Sofa and bathroom furniture were given to a friend. Other furniture went to The Salvation Army.

It was traumatic to let so much go.

Then there were the clothes and all the kitchen stuff. I did five car boot sales before the move and another three since the move. Anything not sold went to the tip or charity shops. At least 20 bags of clothes went to charity and lovely stuff to my local theatre for costumes and props.

There you go, a long list of ideas to help you declutter.

It wasn't just a case of letting stuff go, although that was important. It was knowing how to use what I had, and also deciding what to buy. I moved into my new house and was traumatised and panicky. I still had so much stuff and much of it was old and tatty. I planned to redecorate but had no idea where to start. I was then inspired and an angel visited me in the shape of Jane – architect and interior designer.

Valuable lesson: if you are overwhelmed don't be frightened to consult a professional. They will always take the emotion out of life challenges that you face.

Jane sat me down and asked a couple of very simple questions. And no, "What colour would you like your curtains?" was not one of them. She asked me to talk about my life, what I did, what I wanted to do, and how I wanted to live in my house. Jane listened to me for over four hours.

She took notes, asked other questions like: "What items of furniture do you love and want to re-use? Is there anything in particular you would like to have?" Jane wisely realised that I am aspirational and wanted to furnish my house in a way that would suit the life I wanted to have, not the life I had had before. During those four hours I came to see, through Jane's eyes, how this new house could become a beautiful home and working environment.

Clear out

This chapter is a biggy, lots to do in here – you may wish to take a couple of weeks. People vary in their clutter-clearing approach; some people like to take a day and do the whole lot, others prefer to do a little at a time.

You are going to tackle the clothes, furniture and stuff in your home first.

In order to change you will need to let go of the items that remind you of the old negative beliefs about yourself and how you relate to others. Clear out your surroundings in the same way that you have cleared out your brain code.

Ladies and Gentlemen – let's go looking for your superhero gear. Open those wardrobe doors!

I recommend the following process but do feel free to adapt.

You will need five bags or boxes:

- ☐ *A keep pile.*
- ☐ *A car boot/eBay/Gumtree pile.*
- ☐ *A charity shop bag.*
- ☐ *Rags for recycling (socks, knickers and vests are great dusters).*
- ☐ *And a dustbin bag or ten.*

Leave the goodies you are keeping and selling on their hangers or folded nicely. Charity shops will not take stuff on hangers. Some of you will not be bothered with selling on – fair enough, stick them into the charity pile.

Before you start clearing I want you to really raise your energy and tune into your dream life. Close your eyes and listen to the recording you made about your vision of how you want your business day to be, read the words you wrote. Take at least 15 minutes of breathing slowly and calmly and reflecting on how you want to be when you are working and meeting people, when you are being your amazing self.

Ladies, when I was asked by my coach to clear out my wardrobes, she gave me some great advice. She said: "Only keep the clothes that will allow you to do the following: as you get dressed in the morning imagine the man of your dreams is sitting downstairs waiting for you. Dress to ensure he decides to take you out for the day." I dress for Harry Connick Jr. every morning! OK, sometimes I work on the basis he's not wearing his specs that day. Folks, you could dress for your ideal clients. Either way, have a clear idea of what you wear now that you are living your dream.

Then put on some great music or the radio and DO IT! Look at each item – does your successful self wear this? How do you feel when you wear it? If the item does not help you feel great, then it goes. Incidentally, I asked my coach what I should wear when cleaning the house or doing the gardening. And her reply was: "A gorgeous outfit with dungarees on top!" Between you and me, I have kept the gardening clothes, but I would never wear them where I might be seen by potential clients. Although that is not the point. The objective is to become the person you dream of becoming as much as you can, as soon as you can. For me that means being beautiful and groomed at all times. What does it mean for you?

Guys – who are your clients? Do they include women? Women love crisp collared shirts, trousers with belts, the occasional gorgeous tie and smart, lovely shoes.

Girls – think heels, no matter your height. I am just under six foot tall, I have been terrified of wearing heels all my life. But hey! If you have to look up at me anyway, what difference are a couple of inches going to make? I'll tell you the difference. It makes me feel as if I stand out. It makes my adrenalin pump a little faster, apparently wearing heels does do that. I have to believe I am a gorgeous woman and act that way, because I sure can't hide. And that works for you delicious five-footers too.

You need to feel a little scared of your outfit. Just like a superhero costume you need to live up to your clothes. Start sorting and chucking: clothes, shoes, accessories, underwear – especially underwear. Remember what your gran told you about being run over. Would you be happy for that tasty doctor to see you in your undies? (note that applies to men and women!) The gorgeous Joanna Lumley said that the one rule she follows is to be clean – top to toe, under to outer.

Get help to go through your wardrobe if you need, but not necessarily from your life partner. Employ a makeover professional, or ask a friend who thinks like your ideal client.

You may only have one suit left, one pair of decent shoes. That's OK. When you go shopping again, invest. Would the super-successful you wear those £40 shoes? If not, don't buy them. Don't compromise; you will always know that you did and it will affect your confidence.

Many of you will be saying: "But I don't wear suit and tie, or heels, because I am a personal trainer." (Or a beauty therapist or a…) Understood. So have a uniform for being your successful self which is smart and clean and sassy. And when you are out of uniform and out and about, you wear what you would wear if you were your dream self, off work!

The point is made?

Environment declutter

It's now time to clear the clutter in your surroundings. This book is about having a successful business, so have a look at your working environment. For many of you your working environment will be your home.

First step: Immerse yourself in your dream day again. What does your dream business environment look like? To what extent can you create that for yourself now? Do you have a space that is your work space? Is it clear and clean and calming? Are you able to bring clients there? Do you have space that allows you to focus when you are on the phone?

Second step: Whether or not you bring clients to your office or workshop, keep it as if you do. Your clients may never see your work environment, but you will always feel better knowing that if they did, it is clean and shiny, just like your undies. Furnish it with the furniture and items that support and enhance your dream. Lose the stuff that pulls you back and brings you down. Create an environment that inspires you.

Clear the head clutter

Here are some ideas that will help support the decluttering of your head.

Think about how you start your day. What will your ideal self eat for breakfast? Remember, in your dream you are as slim and healthy as you want to be. What is your dream breakfast? Is it going to give you the nourishment you need to use your superpowers? Changing the food you eat can be an easy and inexpensive way to becoming the person you dream of being.

Let's go back to before breakfast. How could you 'rise and shine'? To quote Hitch in the movie: "Start each day as if it's on purpose." I know many of you have children, or start work very early. But I encourage you to try introducing some or all of the following into your morning routine.

- *When you awaken, lie quiet for a few minutes and think about the events you are looking forward to doing during the day. Feel how happy you are going to be, smile and enjoy the anticipation of that fulfilled happiness.*

- *A journal. Declutter your brain by writing down your thoughts and concerns. Write your plans for the day, your things to achieve. Write down your dreams and your prayers. Unload your anger, fears and frustrations. Write at least three sides of paper.*

- *Have an affirmation, a positive statement about you, your dream, how you want to be. Say it aloud, several times, preferably into a mirror. Write it down several times. Pin it up on your fridge, or where you will see it.*

- *Girls, make time to have a relaxing bath every morning. Women need to bathe as early as they can in the day. It is your chance to replenish your loving energy by allowing yourself to feel loved, at peace and calm. A shower is enjoyable but not the same; more practical, less lovingly luxurious.*

- *Meditate, maybe in the bath? Quieten your brain and just be. Allow thoughts to pass through your head, attach balloons to them and let them float away. No questioning, no gnawing away, just accept. Sense your heartbeat in your chest, your hands, your feet. Feel how you are feeling. Don't ask why. Just feel. Be in your body, not in your head.*

- *Include a little exercise. Stretching, yoga, or something more vigorous. Something to energise your body.*

- *Breakfast. Please avoid refined sugar and don't drink tea or coffee with your breakfast. Apparently there is something in tea and coffee which prevents the absorption of any positive mineral nutrients you may have eaten. I am not going to preach at you about your diet, but consider your dream self – what do they eat for breakfast?*

- *Do a little tidying up of your space during this time in the morning. It fulfils the need to 'fetch water, chop wood'.*

- *Then get dressed, tell Harry thanks, but you're busy, and get off to work.*

Clear your procedures of clutter

I am smiling because I am moving into an area where I need to focus and practise to improve. Please remember, folks, life is a journey, not a destination. So perhaps we can tackle this area together?!

Is your business a smooth, well-oiled, lean machine? Do you have easy access to the information you need when you need it? Are you busy doing the actions that will make best use of your gifts and delegating the rest? Sometimes we use the everyday clutter of tasks that we feel we should do in order to stop us from doing the tasks that will give the service and bring in the money.

During my BT career I had great fun for a few days doing a time and motion study on the engineers, the people that fitted telephone lines, went up poles and down holes. I followed after them with a clipboard noting what they did and how much time they spent on it. There was an allocation code, e.g. travel, paperwork, installation work are some examples. What became obvious very quickly is that where there was a supportive structure and process in place, time can be spent in ensuring that the customer facing work is done well, politely and appropriately. But where the process has not been maintained correctly, i.e. incorrect address or ill-maintained records, time is spent away from income-earning activities. That's when customers and engineers become less, um, polite.

Are you ready to do a time and motion study? Just kidding. Wouldn't that be fun, spending days doing a TMS instead of working on what you already suspect? Anyway, I already did one at BT for you. There is a universal rule in place that you can apply to everything and it is great for decluttering. You will have heard of it. The Pareto rule: the 80:20 rule.

Let me give you some examples.

It is likely that you spend 80% of your customer time serving 20% of your customers.

It is likely that 20% of your customers bring you in 80% of your income. By the way, it's also very likely that they are not the same 20% that are taking up your time.

You probably spend 80% of your working day doing stuff that will not directly serve customers and earn you income.

AC SEN CHU ATE the positive, eliminate the negative, don't mess with Mr In Between

Let me explain: if 'my' Pareto rule is on track, 80% of you are considering becoming, or are already, solo-preneurs running your own businesses.

The purpose of this exercise is to help you look at ways to declutter your business processes. Your own mini time and motion study.

Write down the actions in your business that *you* are responsible for doing. These are the actions that find you clients and serve those clients in a way that brings you income. In effect you are writing your job description.

Write down what only *you* can do within your business.

For a simplified example, in my business, my role is:

- *Communicating the services I offer (promotion, communication).*
- *Writing and designing the material (creating).*
- *Defining the value of the material and price (pricing and packaging).*
- *Delivering the service (speaking, coaching) when the price has been paid (fulfilment of the agreement).*
- *Listening to clients, adapting, ensuring they feel they are getting value (customer care).*
- *Now, if I do the above 80% of my working time, I reckon my business will do well. That should be your objective.*

_____

_____

_____

_____

Now that you have a list of your key actions, the tasks that move you and your business forward, you can aim to be doing these 80% of your working time.

As a supplement activity to this have a look at your diary. Challenge each task that you do and think whether you need to do it or whether you can get it resourced elsewhere.

Have a think about how you are spending your day. It is easy to get distracted by the clutter. What can you drop?

What can you delegate? What can you adjust? Think about your superhero persona. How does she fill her day? Yes, she is responsible for delivering a service and getting income for it, but she does not have to send out every invoice and chase it up.

Have fun, be creative. As you do something ask yourself: "How is this helping my extraordinary business? And do I need to do it, or could someone else?"

Highlights

CHAPTER FIVE
Clear your clutter

- ✓ *Clutter is the stuff, both physical and mental, that clouds or bars the way to change.*
- ✓ *If we do as we have done we shall be as we have been; change lies in that which we avoid.*
- ✓ *Clutter includes old commitments, negative people, procrastination, things around you that are not beautiful or useful, including clothes and accessories.*
- ✓ *Clutter also includes long-winded processes, irrelevant tasks, impractical support systems.*
- ✓ *Remember the dream business day, how you look and what you do during that day. Start to introduce changes into your life that will get you closer to the dream.*
- ✓ *Look at your business processes and consider where you could make them leaner.*
- ✓ *Map the customer lifecycle, think about how you can focus 80% of your time on your customers, and delegate other tasks.*

Activities:

- ☐ **Declutter your wardrobe, environment, head, process - page 60**
- ☐ **ACT SEN CHU ATE the positive – page 67**

CHAPTER SIX
Clarify your vision for your business

The story so far...

Our heroine, that's you, has lived an amazing life full of adventures, love, heartbreak, happiness, unhappiness and has arrived safely to this point in her life and is exactly the person that she is supposed to be, with all of the requisite experience and qualifications. This she knows because she has recorded them.

Our heroine realises that she has superhuman abilities and secret weapons and that there is no one else like her in the world.

And our heroine has a dream of how she would like her life to be. She dreams of the castle, the prince, the happy faces of the people she helps and the ever-flowing gold in the cellar (or is that the wine?).

She knows that she has Herculean tasks ahead of her in order to achieve her dreams and she is already well on the way to beheading her first monster. At least she knows which outfit and shoes she'll be wearing to do the deed.

And possibly the chariot, or charger, she'll be using too! She also knows that she has cleared space in her castle for the happy people she serves, the gold, the prince and the kids, the wine and anything else in her dreams. This is because she has done a thorough declutter in order to clear the way for her dreams to come true, at least 80% of the time.

Which, if you are dreaming of the stars, will get you at least as far as the moon, and that's not a bad payback on a dream.

The next step takes a bit of planning, logic and realism. Serious left brain stuff so you may need the ruler and calculator along with the coloured pens and the mind maps!

It's time to start creating your own reality. Well, to be fair, you have been doing that all your life. But you probably were not aware of how powerful you are. Just like Mickey Mouse in Disney's *The Sorcerer's Apprentice*, you have been wielding the magic wand with the objective of cleaning the kitchen and you've ended up with smashed plates and a mop in your face.

Remember though, every so often in your life the magic *has* happened. You found the love of your life. Your babe smiled at you with love. You got the job. You grabbed the best parking space. You won the Lottery. Your Yorkshire puddings rose. You came first. These are all examples of the magic you will be using to create your dream. Eh? Yes, the one superpower we all share is the magical ability to make our dreams come true. Sadly perhaps, it takes most of us a good few years to recognise that we are all Apprentice Sorcerers. The good news is you have started to make the magic happen and it's all going to be OK.

You have a dream of how you would like your business life to be. This chapter is all about building a structure around the dream. It will also give you an opportunity to check that your dream is truly aligned with you and how you want to live your life.

You are going to create a Vision and Mission. That may sound high falutin' but if you don't know where you want to be, how will your magic work? Remember Mickey? He didn't focus on clearing the kitchen mess, he got carried away with having fun and chaos ensued. Don't worry, your Business Vision and Mission will keep you on the straight and narrow.

Definition of Business VISION:

A Vision Statement defines what a business will do and how it will be, in the future. It is a business statement defining the founder's dream.

Ask yourself the following questions in order to help you define your Vision:

- *How do I want my business to be in the future?*
- *Why is my business here?*
- *How do I want my business to look?*

A Vision Statement is brief. It shapes your understanding of why you are in business, and remains constant while you are in business. It is inspirational.

MISSION definition: Your Mission Statement describes what you do every day in order to achieve your Vision. It answers the 'What do you do?' question. Think Big Hairy Audacious Goals.

There are, of course, many business references that will help you define and write these statements. Take a look on the internet to get some ideas. I did.

Example:

BT: *Our vision is to be dedicated to helping customers thrive in a changing world.*

(Perfect – answers the Why is BT here? question)

Our mission is to be the leader in delivering converged networked services.

(Simply explains what BT does)

Sky

At Sky, we believe in better. Better technology, better programmes and better customer service are what have made us Britain and Ireland's leading entertainment and communications company. Believing in better also helps to ensure that what we do benefits society as a whole, as well as our customers and shareholders. This is the Vision behind the bigger picture.

> **Approach:**
>
> At Sky, we put our customers at the heart of everything we do, investing in stand-out programming and innovative products. We look to the long term, making sure we are a responsible business day to day, inspiring our customers to make a positive difference to society, and ensuring Sky is a great place to work.

Most major companies publish their Mission and Vision Statements because of the importance of expressing their purpose and function, and how they are going to fulfil them, to their clients. It is integral to branding and helps us, as customers, decide whether we resonate with a company's culture, or not.

> **Sue Vizard Vision**
>
> I will expand in success, love and abundance every day by showing those around me that they are each uniquely gifted. That when we tune into and use our extraordinary abilities we can have dream lives and businesses, having fun loving what we do for clients we love.
>
> OK – needs work. But it inspires me and that's what counts.

Sue Vizard Mission Statement

I will achieve my Vision by:

Writing motivational, loving, informative, practical and useful books, and other learning materials, for people who run their own businesses throughout the world.

Living and working in a way that is congruent with my teaching in order to show integrity and my belief that a great life and business is possible.

Using every opportunity to share my knowledge, experience and tools with people who have expressed interest in working with me.

Shining, designing and refining my approach and material as I learn through experience and intuition how I can better give loving motivation and information to support my clients.

Define Your Vision

Close your eyes and reflect on your dreams for your life and your business life. Ask yourself the following questions in order to help you define your Vision:

- *Where do I want my business to be in the future?*
- *Why is my business here?*
- *What is it about my service that inspires me?*
- *How do I want people to feel about my product?*
- *What results will I deliver?*

Note the answers to these questions, string the answers together, and then edit them until you have a Vision Statement that inspires and challenges you. It is perfect if it makes you feel nervous and sweaty.

___

___

___

If you can dream it – you can do it.

WALT DISNEY

Write Your Mission Statement

The Mission Statement describes what the business does in the present in order to achieve the Vision (in the future). The Mission Statement is often structured as a list of goals.

Write statements starting 'I will achieve my Vision by...' then edit them until they become a series of statements that are congruent with your Vision and challenging for you.

___

___

___

Remember Mission goals can be adjusted as the environment that your business is in changes and as they are achieved. Your Mission should always be in line with your Vision and that remains a constant. Of course you may rewrite your Vision Statement but the essence, the dream, remains.

Ensure also that your Vision and Mission Statements challenge you. Face up to those lingering negative voices about your abilities. Say thank you for their concern but they belong to a different time and situation. These are your dreams we are talking about here – I expect them to be Big, Hairy, Audacious, Monster Dreams, in 3D with moving blue fur and big teeth!

Values

The thesaurus states that values are principles, ethics, standards of behaviour.

Please have a think about your values. What is important to you about how you do your business? Actually what is important to you about how you live your life? What values will you instil into the framework of your business? So much so that you employ people because they demonstrate the same values as you, and you look for clients that have the same values. Values become so integral to you and your business that you could not deliver your service in any other way.

> Jane, the interior designer, values trust. She works on communicating with her client in order to foster an environment of mutual trust. Without that trust element Jane cannot progress with her work. She is going to invest time, energy and money in work for her client; she needs to trust that her client has been honest with her about their requirements and ability to pay. The client trusts Jane with her property, often providing Jane with a key and allowing her to bring strangers into the house.

> Jonathan, my IFA, values integrity. As I passed his contact details to a friend the other day I told her he 'reeked of integrity'. Ooops – perhaps reeking is not the most positive word! But Jonathan will tell you the situation as he sees it, warts and all. He will do what he said he will do, and he will ensure that you understand why he is doing what he is doing. He will show you the workings out – if that's what you want. If a product is not right for you, he will tell you. Ooh, and he wants to make money, but not at the expense of his integrity. I like that in an IFA!

If you are still not sure what your values are, ask your current clients, or friends. You may be surprised at what they think your values are.

> **Sainsbury's**
> **Our values**
>
> Our five values provide the framework for how we do business at Sainsbury's. They guide us in everything we do – from key business decisions to day-to-day activities.
>
> - *Best for food and health.*
> - *Sourcing with integrity.*
> - *Respect for our environment.*
> - *Making a positive difference to our community.*
> - *A great place to work.*

I think this excerpt from the Sainsbury's website states very clearly what their values are and how important they are to the Sainsbury business. A good example of a Values Statement.

My values are:

enthusiasm, respect, positivity, adding value, friendliness, integrity, responsibility, congruency, acceptance and ongoing learning and personal development.

Have a bit of fun – who are your favourite companies? Why don't you go and look at their values. Do they ring true? Perhaps that's why you like shopping with them. Your clients may never see your Values Statement but it is important that your business 'reeks' of your values and those who work with you have the same values.

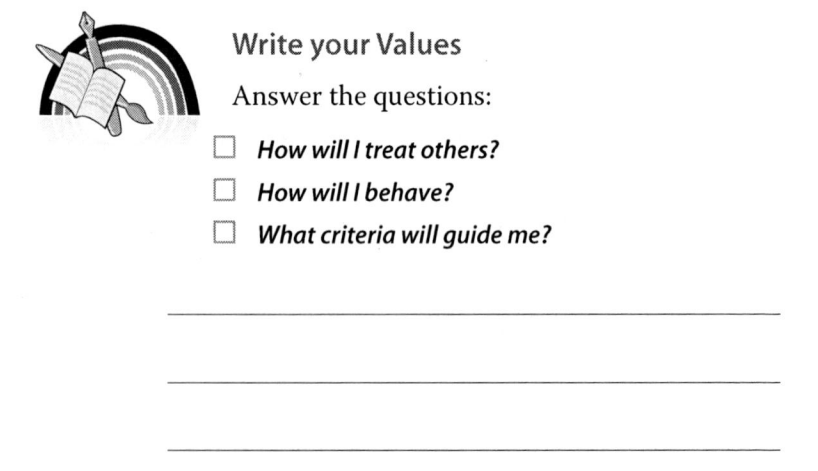

Write your Values

Answer the questions:

- ☐ *How will I treat others?*
- ☐ *How will I behave?*
- ☐ *What criteria will guide me?*

_____

_____

_____

Why is writing your Vision, Mission and Values a vital action?

Because your dream now has a structure and momentum in order to achieve future objectives. Doesn't everything begin to click into place?

To carry on the Sorcerer's Apprentice analogy – you now know what it is you want to achieve. You know what it looks like, how it will benefit others and, most importantly, how it will benefit you. You know, at a very high level, what you need to do now, and every day, in order to get there. You also know how you will behave, and to what standard.

That's you with your wand, your magic hat, knowing what you want to achieve and even an idea of the words to say in the spell. Point your wand, Mickey, and have faith the magic will work. Live each day as if the magic is working and it will.

The Law of Attraction

Many of you will have read or seen *The Secret* by Rhonda Byrne and some may be sceptical about the Law of Attraction. Although it seems a little 'woo woo', there is some science behind the theory – quantum physics apparently. Everyone and everything are bundles of energy particles magically held together by, well, an energy force that is strong enough to hold us together: vibrational attraction. Energy vibration attracts particles that vibrate at the same level.

Now that you have a Vision that you can feel, breathe and live within, have complete faith that through your actions you can make your Vision reality. The magic begins to happen, the Law of Attraction will kick in and you will attract the particles you desire and visualise towards you, in the form of abundance. That may be a little 'out there' for you but please believe that the universe is a magical place and that we are here to live fulfilled joyful lives, loving and being loved, and that the universe is generously abundant. We are born innocent and ready to live those lives, but the tragedy is that many are unconscious of this and learn other beliefs of pain and anger and failure which influence them throughout their lives.

You have already shown you are a dreamer. You have already shown that you are prepared to serve yourself and other people with your contribution to life through your business. Now that you have shaped your dream, you have done the hard part. Live your dream and trust in abundance and your energy. Your focused thought and 'in tune living' will become like a magnet for people and opportunities that will support your Vision and Mission. I promise you that when you wave your wand and believe in your abracadabra, your buckets will get in line, your brooms will stand to attention and the water will begin to flow and bubble. I can't promise you that it will be immediate, although I do believe that the simpler the request the quicker the universe will manifest it for you. Go on, try manifesting a parking space. You will be astounded at how often that works.

Even if you think this Law of Attraction stuff is a load of hogwash, you have to admit that it helps to have a clear Mission and Vision. Something to put on your website that will help you with your branding and logo. You can make business and life decisions guided by your Mission and Values. Ask yourself: "Will that progress me to my Vision? Yes or no? Does that match my Values?" You cannot help but move towards your Vision and therefore you pull the fulfilment of your dream closer to you.

You have now created the Vision and Mission and Values for your business.

You have done what big corporations spend millions of pounds doing, and you have done it for the same reason: in order that your business has a goal, a purpose and high-level ways of fulfilling those. These are the key items needed to give your business an identity, personality and culture.

Calling in your clients

Now your business has meaning and an identity you can progress to the next steps and begin to communicate with your clients, subtly. Let me explain what I mean.

> **Here is an example for those of you that have children.**
>
> Remember before you were trying for children, you didn't even give prams and pushchairs a second glance? What to eat to help get pregnant, best times of the month, what hospital to use, what birth method to choose? You were totally oblivious to those choices. Yet suddenly, when you are trying for a baby, this huge subterranean world that you didn't even know existed emerges. Like Platform 9 ¾ Kings

Cross opens up to reveal the Hogwarts Train. There you are, the new kid in first year, on a very steep learning curve. There is so much to learn and it's so exciting and you had no idea it was even there! How do you process all of this information?

The metaphor is this.

You dream of having a baby, you visualise a healthy child and a 'best for all' birth – that is your Vision.

As you learn a little more about childbirth you begin to develop your Mission, i.e. how and where you would like the birth to be.

It could be that your Values are such that you do not like to use drugs, so your Mission includes the intention for a drug-free delivery.

Or it could be that you need a caesarean delivery; therefore your Mission is different. Your Vision –that of a healthy baby and problem-free birth – is the same, but your Mission is now to find the best obstetric surgeon, the right hospital facilities etc. If this is your Mission then you do not look at information for home births, or 'midwife-only' delivery.

Do you see that you look for, and draw towards you, the options that are aligned with your Vision, Mission and Values regarding your baby's birth? As you become more focused you will meet people who supply what you are looking for, in the way that you need it. And, just as importantly, you discard the options that are not congruent with your plans.

How about a business example of the importance of the necessary foundations of a Vision, Mission and Values?

Let's imagine Lily, who loves gardening and is thinking of setting up a gardening business, in a town where there are already a quite a few gardeners.

Lily's Vision is to run a business that creates and maintains gardens beautifully and makes her a good living. That could also be the same Vision as other gardeners. However Lily's Values include that she wants to use organic products and be an environmentally aware gardener. Therefore Lily's Mission includes a statement in which she states she doesn't use weedkiller or any chemicals or processes that may damage the environment.

Lily's gardening business will have a different identity from the others, because it is aligned with *her* superpowers, Vision, Mission and Values.

Do you see, deciding and committing to run your business aligned to your Mission, Vision and Values framework will define more closely your potential customer and the message that you transmit? Your business's identity defines your branding and your marketing.

This is when the exciting magic begins.

Highlights

CHAPTER SIX
Clarify your vision

- ✓ *Structuring your dreams will breathe life into them.*
- ✓ *You are the gardener of the seeds of your dreams.*
- ✓ *A Vision Statement answers the 'What will you and your business do/be?' question.*
- ✓ *The Mission Statement describes how you will do it.*
- ✓ *Listing your Values defines your ethics and standards.*
- ✓ *Create your Vision from the statements within your dream.*
- ✓ *Clarifying your Vision will give you momentum and inspiration.*

Activities:

- ☐ **Define your Vision, Mission and Values**
  - pages 76, 77 and 80

CHAPTER SEVEN
Remember what you love about your business

The nature of commitment

I am a fan of musicals and one of my favourite musicals is Fiddler on the Roof. I particularly resonate with it because my great-grandfather's family fled from Russia during the Pogroms in the late 19th century. Incidentally, they were circus performers and theatrical people. Some of them toured with the Barnum and Bailey Circus for several years. No wonder I am so shy and retiring...

For those of you who don't know the story of Fiddler on the Roof, the lead character, Tevye (iconically played by the actor Topol), is the Jewish father of three beautiful daughters. Traditionally their husbands are chosen for them by the Matchmaker. As the family are very poor, the Matchmaker's objective is to find single men with money. Sadly there are not many of them in this little village, and the few who are there are perhaps not a young girl's idea of the ideal husband. Each of the daughters rebels; the first marries a poor Jewish tailor, her dad can just cope with this; the second marries an impoverished communist teacher who takes her far away; and the third, ah the third daughter! Well you will need to watch the film, or see the musical, to find out what happens. I started this example not thinking about tradition, but about commitment. One of my favourite songs, and scenes, is between Tevye and his wife Golde (played in the film by Anne Bancroft). Their marriage was arranged, possibly by the same elderly Matchmaker; they did not marry for love. Tevye asks Golde in this scene if she loves him.

GOLDE: *Do I love you?*
For twenty-five years I've washed your clothes
Cooked your meals, cleaned your house
Given you children, milked the cow
After twenty-five years, why talk about love right now?

TEVYE: *But do you love me?*

GOLDE: *Do I love him?*
For twenty-five years I've lived with him
Fought him, starved with him
Twenty-five years my bed is his
If that's not love, what is?

> **TEVYE:** *Then you love me?*
>
> **GOLDE:** *I suppose I do.*
>
> **MUSIC BY JERRY BOCK,**
> **LYRICS BY SHELDON HARNICK**
>
> And then they both sing: "It doesn't change a thing, but even so, after 25 years, it's nice to know".

This chapter is about commitment – to your dreams, your Business Vision, to what you have decided you want for your life. Which, I hope, is your commitment to a great business, having fun loving what you do, for clients you love, and prospering.

The thesaurus describes *commitment* as: dedication, loyalty, devotion, responsibility, duty, obligation, pledge, promise, guarantee, vow.

Committed: dedicated, devoted, loyal, resolute and pledged, involved, promised, engaged, duty-bound.

I was terrified of commitment. I thought making a commitment was the same as losing my freedom. I think it also had a lot to do with the fear that I would commit myself to the wrong thing and then I would be trapped.

One of the reasons that businesses fail is lack of commitment.

JumpStart *The* Start Up Book *for* your Dream Business

Shirley's story

Shirley succeeded in the corporate world working for an international engineering company; she is an engineer. She was promoted for her management ability and 'masculine' approach. She wore dark suits and understood how to play the power politics required to succeed in that environment. One day she realised that suppressing her 'feminine' abilities and skills was causing her mental and possibly physical pain. She realised she needed to change so she learned Teaching English as a Foreign Language, gave up corporate life, and went to teach in schools in Africa and Asia. Sadly she found herself in pain again, this time in an environment where she was physically as well as emotionally abused. Her imminent marriage to a bully luckily fell through, and she ran to the UK to stay with a friend.

I met Shirley while she was setting up a women's networking group and needed help with promotion and marketing for that group. Shirley threw everything she had at setting up this group, travelled around the country, spent all her money, spoke to everyone, everywhere she could.

At first I didn't identify why women didn't flock to her, because she is charismatic, a born leader and an incredible woman. She was senior in another international networking organisation, and had been for several years.

I began to listen to what she said. She was unhappy with where the group had been set up; it wasn't in the town that she lived in and she mentioned that regularly. She was in financial difficulties and her new networking group was costing her more than it made. She didn't always agree with the preset format for the group and would occasionally do her own thing. That put her at conflict with the network's message which also subtly undermined her commitment to the group. Eventually Shirley left the network and found a full-time job.

As I look back I realise that there were a few things which prevented Shirley's success at this particular initiative. Shirley had been positively changing people's lives, all her life, and continues to do so, I am sure. However, she was not fully committed to this particular network. Her (I believe unconscious) motivation for joining it was to ease her pain, to find a place to share her experiences with loving women, hoping that the pain would disappear in the telling of it. But, if anything, her choice to join the network maintained this pain through her feeling a failure and an outsider.

Many of us work hard and long hours at our business, throwing all our effort, money and resources at it, and it still does not succeed. And that, dear reader, could be because we are not committed, we are not truly in love with ourselves and what we are doing.

So, ask yourself, how do you feel about what you earn money doing? Do you feel trapped by the idea of truly dedicating yourself to one dream?

Perhaps, like me, you fear the pain of failure and so you ensure that you do not take responsibility for your actions and therefore cannot be blamed if you are not successful.

Alternatively, like Shirley, you have a huge sense of loyalty and duty and have given and given to everyone and everything else but yourself. And therefore the thought of continuing to give your all in this way is linked so closely with pain that even the thought of making a commitment is too painful. You become a prisoner to the fear of pain. You are someone who has learned by previous choices, by circumstances, by lack and by fear, to avoid commitment, success and love.

Perhaps commitment can only happen when you realise that you have always been free to choose whether or not to follow that path. That you are not in a cage and, unlike death and taxes, you always have a choice. If you feel that you do not have a choice then there is resentment and resistance, and commitment to the chosen path will not happen. It is your attitude and acceptance of the situation that makes it positive and not the situation itself.

As I write this chapter I recognise I have much to experience about being committed to something. I am trying to write a book that is authentic and congruent with my dream for my life but I am finding this chapter, in particular, very difficult to write.

This book shares with you what I have learned about living a happy and fulfilled business life by following the tools, techniques, beliefs and approaches that I recommend. When the book becomes public, so must my commitment to the book. No more hiding, running away or excuses! It's time to be seen 'walking the talk'.

My resistance to this commitment is monstrous and scary. Today I have wept then run off to speak to someone to get reassurance. I have faffed around doing the washing. I then had a little breakdown and went to sleep for an hour or so. This book is possibly my greatest positive public commitment and as such it will be an outstanding achievement for me. I am so scared and resistant to being the true, honest, powerful me that I am doing all I can to avoid becoming that person.

I am going to write this chapter and finish this book though. You know why? Because my Vision of showing you that you can live your dream life, having fun, being happy, can only come true if I live it and publish my book about it. Easy? No. Simple? Yes.

People and the nature of commitment

Look at Queen Elizabeth II for example. She has made a commitment to reign as Queen, spending her lifetime devoting herself to her subjects.

Another iconic figure displaying the highest commitment is Pope Benedict XVI. And yet, after eight years in office, he became the first pope to resign in hundreds of years. He realised that he was not well enough to fulfil the role as he believes it needs to be fulfilled.

What do these two iconic people show us regarding the nature of commitment?

Choice

Both the Queen and the Pope had a choice whether or not to accept the role. The Queen could have said no, her uncle did. It won't be because of lack of commitment on her part if the UK becomes a republic. Once she decided to become Queen, she chose to no longer have a choice. Queen Elizabeth has wasted no time questioning her decision.

Therefore commitment requires positive decision. It cannot be forced on you. In order to decide to commit to your Vision you need to have freely chosen to jump.

> *You always have two choices:*
> *your commitment versus your fear*
>
> **SAMMY DAVIS JR.**

Faith

Although other people have taken on the role in the past, e.g. being a queen or pope, the person who was the figurehead of the London Olympics, Lord Coe, demonstrated that making a commitment is a leap of faith into the unknown (thank you Lord Coe). No one can tell you how it's going to be for you. Everyone is different.

You need to have faith that you will be enough.

> *Faith is to believe what you do not see; the*
> *reward of this faith is to see what you believe*
>
> **SAINT AUGUSTINE**

Responsibility and Leadership

In writing this book, and sharing ideas and suggestions about how to live your lives, I become a teacher, guide and leader. I take on a role of responsibility which I have been trying to avoid for a long time. My head is above the parapet, there for you to shoot at. Saying 'I stand for this belief' is not enough. I need to be prepared to be challenged. I must live in a way that shows I accept this responsibility.

So must you.

Full Time

Commitment is for life, not just for Christmas. Thank you again Lord Coe for helping me to understand this. Commitment is for all of your life, for the life of the commitment. Queens, popes and Olympic moguls have a Vision. They are committed to achieving their Vision and that rules their lives 24/7. Even when they are resting they are resting within their commitments: no drugs, enough sleep, constant practice. When the Vision is achieved, only then you can lay down that commitment. For some it is when the Olympic Games have been delivered, for others it is lifelong.

Don't settle for less, positively addicted

It seems that once you have flexed that commitment muscle you want to stretch it further. Until you recognise that you no longer have the ability, or you get tired, like Pope Benedict. I'll let you know!

Note to self, add a crown to my superhero costume – or maybe a pope-mobile.

Business Commitment

I *do* understand that commitment is love, faith and belief. Deciding to love is making a commitment. I also believe that happy and successful business people love their clients, and use their gifts to give to their clients. They 'work like they don't get paid'.

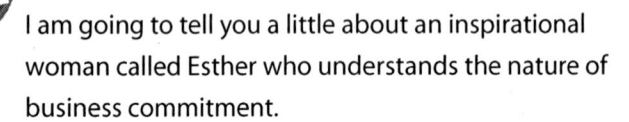

> I am going to tell you a little about an inspirational woman called Esther who understands the nature of business commitment.
>
> I met Esther for coffee a few weeks ago, when I had started to write this book. I wanted to talk with her about marketing as she is a partner in a marketing company, but between you and me, I just wanted to be around her for a little while.
>
> Esther is committed to making a positive difference within her business community. Her superpowers, I believe, are energy, courage and vision, an open mind and the intelligence to apply her learning for her clients' benefit. Esther shared with me her most precious gift, her time. She was generous with her advice, ideas and suggestions. All things that she had every right to withhold for just her clients. That didn't occur to her because Esther is committed to helping others succeed.

CHAPTER SEVEN - Remember what you love about your business

> She also introduced me to 'God' – Seth Godin, The Marketing Guru. (If you care about marketing, look him up. If you care about your business, look him up.) I can see Esther as a world leader, I really can. She gave me another great gift. She opened my eyes to the opportunity and did not question whether or not I would be good enough. Esther said that there are too few people willing to be leaders. At the time I did not recognise what she meant, but instinctively I put her story into this chapter. She meant that there are too few people willing to stick their head above the parapet and be committed to becoming role models, guides, gurus and teachers. She is one and, scarily, so am I. When you truly commit yourself to your business you will become one too.

Business commitment is building your love for your business and having faith in it. It is understanding your superpowers, strengthening them and using them to inspire you and your clients in small steps, every day. And it is bloody hard. But when you see that every challenge you face is an opportunity to shine, refine and recommit – yippee!

Every so often life becomes a grind – difficult and stressful. I have had a bit of that this last day or so. As I write this book I am testing out my theories in order to recreate my business.

Beware panic and fear

Recently I invited some of my clients and business friends to an evening at a lovely local hotel. I had several objectives: to say thank you, spoil them a little and to let them know about the book and my new business, and find a client or two. I had beautiful leaflets designed, did my presentation and no one bought. I had to remind myself that getting a sale wasn't the main objective, true, but I was still disappointed.

The next morning I called my practical business guy, in a panic, with scattergun business ideas that I thought might be more commercial. He recognised my fear and tried to reassure me to stick to my original business idea of asking my newly formed focus group what they thought. I didn't hear him clearly.

I then girded myself and went through the process of phoning each guest and talking to them in order to get their feedback. During the first few calls I was so full of the voices in my head that I just didn't listen to the guests. I was so full of my ideas of what would be good for them I didn't listen to what they wanted.

I then had a 'light bulb' call with another one of my guests and she was positive and supportive and said that she wanted to work with me and asked for a VIP day. When she is ready. My gosh! This lady is telling me what she will buy from me, marketing GOLD, and I still went into the whirling doldrums. I then spent a

> day avoiding facing anybody or anything, allowing procrastination, sabotage, panic. So sad, especially after all the stuff I had written about commitment!
>
> That morning, when I was writing in my journal, it came to me. My business isn't about me, it's about you. It's about how I can serve you.
>
> Your business isn't about you, it's about your clients.
>
> Suddenly I felt brave again and phoned the last of my guests, a lady who is thinking about starting her own business but is a bit confused as to what to do next. I listened to her, we agreed to have a coffee, and she has become a client.

Do you see what I am trying to say? This stuff is not easy, especially when you are new at trying to grasp and explain this commitment concept.

If you are truly committed to your business and beliefs, you understand that you have taken a leap of faith to fulfil a role that no one has ever done like you before. You have a mission and it's not about how you feel, it's all about how those around you feel through contact with you.

Love what you do

> **How alarming! Love what you do.**
>
> Yesterday, late afternoon, when I had stopped writing to go and prepare my tea, the doorbell rang. There was this young man in high vis waistcoat,

big jacket over a suit, with an alarm company's name splattered all over him. And I spotted a fellow salesman.

He nattered about alarms and how much they have changed and I said no thanks because I am scared of alarms and was pleased not to have one. He countered: "Oh yes, you think that and that, but guess what? Our new alarm does this and this, and you don't have to worry about that and that. Oh, and by the way I am here by invitation from Neighbourhood Watch." I laughed and invited him in. I was intrigued to see how he would work his spiel. "You are such a brilliant salesman," I cooed. He didn't like that. "I am not a salesman," he said.

"So what are you then, if you're not a salesman?" I asked him.

It turned out this young man is exceedingly bright. He has two degrees: Chemistry and Law. Chemistry he had studied at St Andrews, same time as Prince William was there.

This talented young man had come down from the Gods to sell me an alarm. Apparently there is no money in Law and he didn't like it anyway. It also turned out that he had a partial photographic memory, which was an affliction.

I told him again he was a good salesman. "But I'm really not a salesman," he said. He then proceeded to prove the exact opposite.

CHAPTER SEVEN - Remember what you love about your business

I asked him what he thought were the most important attributes for a salesman. "Right attitude, right pitch, right product," he replied. He said that he just relaxes and talks to people, tells them how amazing the product is and then waits.

I asked him how he had been recruited and trained. Well, it was like he was becoming a secret agent! The company aims at graduates, entices them with big bucks and then takes applicants on a test day. They accompany a hotshot knocking on doors. My salesman really enjoyed his day – and, oh my gosh! – he thought the direct selling job was easy money! Alleluia! He said he had won a challenge the newbies had been allocated on Edinburgh's main Prince's Street. He was given a piece of paper with his team leader's autograph on it and told to see how much he could sell it for. Our boy sold it to a Chinese tourist, who spoke excellent English, for £50. I was suitably impressed and wanted to know how. "I told him the truth and he knew what he was buying and wanted to help me out!" he explained.

Salesmen are NOT born, they are made. This intriguing sales company recruited a Law and Chemistry double graduate with a positive attitude, who likes people, and then fine-tuned him. They didn't change him, they just helped him see the fun in what he does, encouraging him to use his superpowers.

Now there is a lesson. Having fun and making money, and loving it!

Let's find out what gives *you* a buzz about your business.

Tuned in

Think back over your working life and recall a time when you last felt 'in tune', i.e. when you last felt happy, creative, at peace, just right. As many examples as you like.

For each example follow this format:

Note down the objective of the work you enjoyed doing, and then describe in detail what you did, how you did it, how you prepared to do it, how you felt while you were doing the task, and the result, and your emotional reward. Write it down in full. Try to remember how you felt when you were doing something that helped you feel 'in tune' and happy.

The objective is for you to experience that happy, fulfilled, contented feeling as often as possible. This exercise will help you understand the actions that help you feel this way.

You can tell when it's good because you forget the time. You can tell when it's right because your heart feels right.

_____

_____

_____

_____

It's an age-old adage (try saying that after a few) that we are good at what we love doing, and we love to do what we are good at doing. I would like to hype that a notch and say: "You are great at what you truly love to do and you truly love to give what you are great at."

Bum note

Think about your working day and list all the things within it: the actions you do, the interactions you have, that make you feel unhappy and frustrated. Include in this list the things that you *avoid* doing because they make you feel unhappy and frustrated.

___

___

___

___

___

Now have a look at this list of horrible 'unhappiness causing' actions and ask yourself:

1. *Do these things need to be done?*

2. *Do these things need to be done in a way that makes me unhappy? How could I do these in a way that makes them fun? 'A spoonful of sugar makes the medicine go down'?*

3. *Do I have to do these things?*

For example, you may have written that phoning people in order to sell to them frustrates you. In which case you have a choice:

- *You can employ someone to do it for you.*
- *Not do it.*
- *Or do it in a way that is more enjoyable for you.*

_____

_____

_____

_____

The objective of both of these exercises is to understand what you love to do. Remember the Pareto rule? Try and get yourself to a place where you are loving what you do at least 80% of the time, and reduce the stuff you don't like. Understand why you don't love it: it could be that you are just not very good at it; you recognise that it is not helping you in your business; or you just do not enjoy doing it for whatever reason. Delegate or drop these actions where possible.

It is not good for your health and state of mind to get paid for work that does not bring you spiritual reward of some kind. If you cannot find joy in most of the work you do you will feel pain.

Do more of the tasks and activities that you enjoy. Adjust your work so that those joyful endeavours become your key business deliverables in order to 'do what you love, loving what you do'.

Highlights

CHAPTER SEVEN

Remember what you love about your business

✓ *Your business needs your commitment in order to succeed.*

✓ *Commitment is for life, not just for Christmas.*

✓ *Commitment with joy, love and choice is freedom.*

✓ *When you commit to something you become a leader, you have put your head above the parapet on behalf of yourself and your business.*

✓ *Do what you love and love what you do as much as possible because therein lies your business success.*

✓ *Understand what you love to do and why and do more of that in the same way.*

✓ *Understand what you dislike to do, and why, and aim to adjust those tasks – either to remove or delegate them or perform them in a different way, in a way that makes them more fun to do.*

Activities:

☐ **Tune in - page 102**
☐ **Bum note – page 103**

CHAPTER EIGHT

Learn to truly love your clients

Getting to know you,
Getting to feel free and easy
When I am with you,
Getting to know what to say.

Haven't you noticed
Suddenly I'm bright and breezy?
Because of all the beautiful and new
Things I'm learning about you
Day by day.

Richard Rodgers and Oscar Hammerstein

The King and I

Dear reader, by now you should be grinning ear to ear and practising leaping tall buildings in a single bound. You realise how extraordinary you are, and if you haven't adjusted a few things in your life then why are you still reading this book? There are no rude bits and we passed the only swear word yonks ago! So maybe you are finding some stuff useful? A little bit, maybe?

At the beginning of the book I made you a promise: that you can have a great life and business (tick) have fun loving what you do (tick) and have great clients.

It's time to introduce you to the people who are going to help you build your business: your clients.

Some of you will be saying "No problem, I can do that, I'm a people person!" Yes, and so am I but being friendly and gregarious are not the skills useful to learn when it comes to 'loving your client'. Quiet people often have crowds of adoring, paying customers. Humans evolved with two ears and one mouth. Listening is twice as vital for effective communication as speaking.

Why is it important to love your clients? Because when you love your clients they will sense that and come back for more, everyone loves to be loved.

Loving your clients will also change how you feel about your business.

Wherever you go you take you with you

I heard this story a long time ago, it may be Buddhist.

There was once a woman who sat on a bucket at the side of the road. The road was on the brow of a hill and stretched from the town in the valley at the bottom of the hill, past the woman and off into the rest of the world to other villages, towns and cities.

It was from this direction that a younger woman appeared, pulling her beautiful wheelie luggage behind her. The young woman stopped by the older woman, pulled out a bottle of water, took a much-

CHAPTER EIGHT - Learn to truly love your clients

needed drink. The old woman said: "Hello, are you travelling to the town in the valley?" The traveller said: "Yes I am. Please tell me, what are the people like in this town?" The old woman asked: "What were the people like in the town you came from?" "Well," said the traveller, "they were mean and rude, thoughtless and sloppy, never paid on time and never invited me in for a coffee." "Ah," said the old woman, "I think you will find the people in this town are exactly the same." The traveller sighed and tutted, tugged on her beautiful luggage and passed the old woman on her way to the town in the valley.

The old woman continued sitting on her bucket at the side of the road until another young woman appeared along the road from the rest of the world, wheeling her beautiful luggage. She stopped by the side of the old woman, smiled and took out two bottles of water, handed one to the old woman. The old woman said: "Hello, are you travelling to the town in the valley?" And the traveller said: "Yes I am. Please tell me, what are the people like in this town?" The old woman asked: "What were the people like in the town you came from?" "Well," answered the traveller, "they were kind and generous, hardworking and thoughtful, always paid on time and loved to take time to chat and have a cuppa." "Ah," said the old woman, "I think you will find the people in this town are exactly the same." The traveller smiled and laughed, tugged on her beautiful luggage and passed the old woman on her way to the town in the valley.

109

Loving your clients will change how you feel about your business, and that will change your life. You will feel motivated to give them your best you.

> **Water cooler**
>
> Piero has lent me a water machine. It's designed for small offices but Piero has one in his home and thinks that I would like it too. He is right, and do you know why he is right? Because Piero has taken time to talk with me.
>
> The machine is smart and provides hot water whenever I want it. I don't have to keep re-boiling the kettle. The cold water is delicious because it is filtered. It may cost more in electricity, I don't know. What I do know is that through Piero's thoughtfulness and 'love' for me I feel that I would like to become part of his customer family, and stay looked after, with this great machine, when the trial runs out. If I decide not to keep it, I will still feel grateful and will be a positive advocate for Piero's business.

Let's define a little further the phrase 'learn to truly love your clients'.

'Learn'? You are an apprentice, as we all are, and every day you commit again to loving yourself a little more than you did yesterday and love those in your world. The fantastic thing is that there is no pressure, none, because you are always learning. And as you understand more what feels right and what feels wrong about what you do, you will trust your intuition more and feel more confident about what actions to take.

And 'truly love'?

True love

Take five minutes to note down some words or actions that describe how you show your love to the ones you love.

_____

_____

_____

True love for *my* client is about accepting who they are, valuing their gifts, listening to what they say and checking that I have understood them. Treating them with respect and taking time to build trust.

> **The power of listening**
>
> Jane, the woman who has transformed my home, initially performed a needs analysis in order to understand what I wanted. Jane could have just brought a series of wallpaper books and asked me what colours I liked. That's not what she did. Jane asked me to explain how I wanted to use my home. She wanted to understand my life, style and aspirations. She asked who would be living in and visiting the house. Then she asked what pieces of furniture and items I would like to have, and what pieces I wanted to keep. She was with me for nearly five hours. As a result I felt listened to, understood, accepted and respected.

Who are 'your clients'?

Your clients are those valuable people who bring, or who could potentially bring, more prosperity into your life.

Take some time now to do a little work in order to identify your ideal clients. Why is this important?

I love this quote: 'Wait, wait, wait for love with the patience of a Buddhist fisherman'. You are going to be Buddhist in the way you call in your clients. You are going to attract them, as a fisherman attracts fish. This is not as passive as it sounds, however it is a little more relaxed than the frantic way that many businesses go about grabbing clients.

How does a fisherman go about fishing?

Firstly he gathers a little knowledge about different types of fishing. Then, based on his interests and experiences to date and his vision of how he would like to fish, he starts to plan. For example, is he a river or sea fisherman? Does he need more experience or training? Can he do this at home or abroad? Who does he know who does this kind of fishing? Is he fishing to eat, for competition, or to throw it back into the water? He narrows down his choices. He decides on where he will fish, how often and with whom.

Then he researches the licences and equipment he will need. It is around this time that he begins to think more specifically about the fish he is aiming to catch. What size are they? What do they eat? What do they look like? When are the best times of year and day to find them? What rods, nets, hooks etc. will be needed? What clothes and footwear will he wear? What bait will attract the fish he wants to catch? Are there other types of fish in the river? For example, ones that he is not licensed for, or interested in catching. How does he attract his fish and discourage the other fish? What competition is there for his fish? Where do his fish like to go? Are there lots of other fishermen there making the area more expensive or over fished? Can he find his target fish anywhere else? Perhaps a little further afield which may incur expenses but there is less competition.

Finally, he is at the riverside and now it is time to fish. He has a pretty good idea how many he wants to catch. Now he learns how to bait the hook, how to cast the line, and how far. He experiments with how often to recast the line. Then he is still. He watches and learns, but waits. He doesn't go chasing after the fish. He doesn't make a lot of noise. He doesn't throw in a huge net and pull up everything in the river, only to throw it all back again. No, our fisherman watches, adjusts things slightly and waits, waits, waits.

You are going to learn how to fish for clients.

Fish defining

You have already written your Business Mission, Vision and Values. These decisions will define what kind of 'fishing' you enjoy, the time you are going to spend doing it and how you are going to do it. You may have defined what product and/or service you are going to offer. Take some time now to understand your target fish in more detail.

Firstly – list all of your clients.

List all the ones who have paid you these past 12 months. List their names and how much you have earned from them. If you have too many to list please write down your top 10, for each income stream. If you earn money from companies, name the decision maker. If you rent out property for income, name your tenants, if possible, but understand who they are. Do a different list for each income stream.

If you have not yet started earning money from your business but are working, I would like you to write down your current manager(s) and the person who recruited you. Please also do this for the last job you had, if you are currently unemployed.

Please just think about the people from whom you are gaining income, or have gained income, in the past. People who have shown they value your product or service for them.

As I write this book I am launching a new income stream and redefining my client profile. It is likely that your business will also change over the next year or so. You may wish to launch a new business. Many of you will therefore be saying: "But the clients I have now are not the ones I want; I will have a different client type in the future. I have loads of different clients, they don't have anything in common."

Change is inevitable.

As you can only work with what you know and what you have experienced to date, that is what we will work with. You may have different income streams, e.g. property rental income, dividends, interest, network marketing. If so, focus on those income streams with clients that you can influence. For example, unless you are a fund manager managing your own funds you cannot influence their performance directly. However, if you rent out property it is worth understanding who your tenants are and what they have in common because you can influence the attractiveness of your property.

You now have a list of clients, even if it's just two names that you can work with.

The next step is to understand what your customers have in common, other than you. Maybe you are the only thing they *do* have in common!

Consider and note down answers to the following questions:

- *Where did you meet them?*
- *How did you start working for them? What was the recruitment process?*

- *What service or product did they buy? If it was a service, how many hours and what did you do for them?*
- *Who do they like to be with?*
- *What hobbies and interests do they have?*
- *What clubs, associations do they have?*
- *Who do they aspire to be like?*
- *What do they do?*
- *How old are they?*
- *Are they married? Do they have kids? What sex are they?*
- *What do you like or appreciate about them?*
- *What do they like, appreciate about you?*
- *Note down other things your 'fish' have in common.*

_____

_____

_____

The objective of this exercise is to gain a greater understanding about your clients. Understanding what it is about you, and them, that has encouraged you to give to them, and them to value that service and pay for it, will help you define your future clients.

Being clear about who you wish to bring into your life, and expressing that, *will* result in those people coming into your life. If you are unhappy because you do not like the people you work with, you have two choices: you accept them as they are or you get out. Bear in mind that you cannot change or control anyone other than you, and attempting to do so will cause you pain.

OK, you have a clearer idea of the clients you are currently able to catch. You know your current fishing experience and skill level. Did you learn anything else? Are you surprised by how effective you are already at 'client catching'? It's a good place to start.

I asked one of my clients who her ideal client was and she described one, but she seemed unenthusiastic, so I asked her who had been her most valuable client. She described her most valuable client and explained that more of this type of client, even if it was just two or three a year, would be what she would like. So she is now focusing on attracting some more of those people, with a great deal more enthusiasm.

Plan for the future ideal client

Think about how and where you want your business to be in one to three years' time (use your Vision and Mission). Who will your ideal client be? That is where you aim your sights. If you plan to have a few streams of income, describe your ideal client type for each stream. Feel free to note down your average income from them. Why not? It will help for your business planning.

You are going to study these people, in order to get to know them. Get clear in your mind who they are, answer the questions in the previous exercise in order to help you with that. Describe them as you would a character in a book. Cut out pictures from magazines of people who look like your ideal client or images of places they might go and things they might do.

This work is preparation in advance of you fishing for these ideal customers.

FOWTW

Know what you want

The business guru, Keith Cunningham, tells a story of how he met his second wife. Keith is a multi-millionaire twice over. He lost his first millions and his business in a property crash.

He had met his second wife while he was running his first business, she used to come in and sell him advertising space in a magazine. He had people who could arrange that for him, but he just liked to be around her, so he would invite her into the office to chat. He was married at the time so nothing untoward happened. He just thought that this saleswoman was gorgeous and he liked to be around her.

When his business crashed and his marriage broke down he became a loner and quietly rebuilt the abundance in his life. One day a few years later, a friend of Keith's called him saying that he knew a lady who would be perfect for Keith – would he like to meet her? Eventually Keith agreed to meet her and guess who it was? That's right, the beautiful advertising space saleswoman. They went out for dinner and they were getting on really well so Keith asked her a key question. No, not that one – Keith is a

> gentleman! Keith said that he would like to become her husband but he wanted to check with her that he was the right man for the job. He then asked her what she wanted in a husband. And she, smart lady, had thought about this and proceeded to tell him. He got out a notebook and wrote it all down – apparently it was a long list! He said that he could meet her requirements, would she marry him? And she said yes.
>
> She was with him at the conference where I heard him speak, and I was lucky enough to say hi briefly. They are such a happy couple and Keith explained that he constantly checks that he is giving his wife what she wants from him as a husband, including a love note every day, even if he is far away.
>
> This story applies to customers as well as life partners.

The multi-millionaire and business guru, Keith Cunningham, explains that there are three rules to follow for a successful business, any business. He uses these acronyms to help us remember:

- *FOWTW*
- *GAGI*
- *GITT*

The first one is what you, as a supplier of goods or services for money, need to do, every day you are in business.

FIND OUT WHAT THEY WANT – and in this section we will look at some tools in order to do that.

(See if you can guess what GAGI and GITT stand for!)

Example

Remember Lily, the gardener who likes to use environmentally friendly, organic methods? Lily has done some research into her ideal client. She has had a chat with a few people and collated a few statements and questions that reflect what her ideal potential client may want from Lily and her gardening business (FOWTW). Here they are:

- *I need a gardener but I don't want chemicals all over the place because of my cat.*
- *How do I find a gardener?*
- *What if the gardener wants to work every week? I am not sure I need that.*
- *How much would a gardener charge?*
- *Will I have to be at home when the gardener comes round?*
- *How will I know if she is a good gardener?*
- *I don't know anyone with a gardener that they recommend.*
- *Shall I go and ask the gardeners that drive the van I see and ask them? What if they are unfriendly?*
- *Can I call the gardener after work?*
- *Will I need to supply gardening equipment or will they bring their own?*

There you have the beginnings of a list of customer issues our eco-friendly gardener could be facing. Can you see how valuable this is?

Walk in your client's shoes

Find a pal, maybe someone who has their own business too, and do some role play. It could be fun, stop groaning!

After the work you have already done you have a clearer idea of who your ideal client is.

Now – arm your pal with pen and paper. You are going to pretend to be your perfect potential client and you are going to moan and mention all the problems and potential issues relevant to your business type that they may be facing, just like Lily's list above, while your pal makes a note of them and adds suggestions too. Then you can swap roles.

_____

_____

_____

_____

Don't lose this work – you will need it for the next chapter, as well as for your business!

Alarm story – FOWTW

As previously mentioned, I talked to an alarm salesperson last week.

The alarm company people he works for have a clear idea of their ideal client, and have Found Out

What They Want. They have considered their ideal customer's issues and addressed them in order to develop the product that was being promoted door to door. This new alarm is obviously the result of serious marketing investment from product development to sale. They will have used focus groups, customer feedback and common sense in order to understand what their client wants. This is what you are doing with these exercises but at a much lower financial investment.

It turns out that the company's ideal client will already have an alarm. Therefore their face-to-face sales team knock on doors of houses with alarms on walls first. Surely it would make more sense to sell to an unalarmed house? Not at all. The potential customer has already accepted that a burglar alarm is necessary, so no need to readdress that concern. She loves the concept of an alarm but, for some reason, does not like the alarm she already has. This new alarm is specifically designed and marketed to clients like her.

The features being promoted include:

- *A pet-proof sensor; pet owners tend not to turn their alarm on in case the cat sets it off.*
- *An alarm which is louder inside the house rather than outside; it's common knowledge that neighbours don't call the police if they hear an alarm, so the noise is to annoy the person breaking in.*

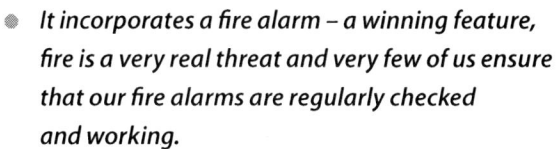

- *It incorporates a fire alarm – a winning feature, fire is a very real threat and very few of us ensure that our fire alarms are regularly checked and working.*

- *24/7 remote monitoring: if the alarm goes off someone in central HQ calls to see whether help is needed. If there is no reply to the call they send someone to the house, including the fire service if it's the fire alarm.*

As you can tell, once the alarm salesperson gets a chance to talk to their *ideal client*, the alarm more or less sells itself.

You can do this too.

Ideal client – Sainsbury's experience

When I was in Sainsbury's the following day I was accosted in the aisle by a sales chap. He carried a well-worn clipboard and card; this man worked hard and knew his stuff. I could tell I was going to be reeled in, but as I was writing this chapter I was intrigued so decided to listen, learn and enjoy the sales experience. It is strange that these sales experiences occurred over the two days as I was writing this chapter. Trust and life will bring you what you need.

His technique was a little heavy handed but it was nice to have a chat.

What was his technique? Conversation. Asking questions in a friendly way, in order to establish whether I was an ideal client match.

His ideal client shops in Sainsbury's at least couple of times a week. She/he also has and uses their reward card, that's me! Once he had established that, he knew he could present the credit card features that would appeal to me. And again, if the marketing is correct, i.e. the card features address the customer's credit card issues, the card sells itself, more or less.

Which of the ideal client's issues did it overcome? Well, other than the standard free balance transfers and reasonable interest rate, the form was easily completed and, most importantly of all, the client gets payback for shopping in Sainsbury's with reward points that they already know, understand and value.

The department store card ideal client

Within that two-day period, I was approached about a store card when I went to buy a dress for a ball (I think it's my first long dress since my wedding dress!). I only have one store card, and I am very

> loyal. However, I almost signed up for this other store's card when I bought the dress. The girl at the till saw an opportunity: as she had not sold me the dress, she aimed to get her cut from the card sale – sensible. So she asked questions of me, made conversation, made friends by giving me a free gift, in order to assess if I was her ideal client.
>
> Sadly, I was not. I don't shop there regularly so I don't value their reward points. Their card was not designed for me, so although the card's features were competitive it was not what I wanted.

The lesson is: when you understand your ideal client, and address their issues within your product or service, it becomes very easy to sell to your ideal client and very difficult to sell to someone else. And that is **OK!**

Highlights

CHAPTER EIGHT
Learn to love your clients

- ✓ *When you love your clients they will sense that and come back for more.*
- ✓ *Loving your clients will change how you feel about your business.*
- ✓ *You will feel motivated to be your best you.*
- ✓ *Define what actions you believe will be showing your clients you care.*
- ✓ *Remember you are never wrong because you are learning all the time.*
- ✓ *Define who your ideal clients are.*
- ✓ *Consider and understand what they like about you.*
- ✓ *FOWTW.*
- ✓ *Understand their issues and potential problems with your business.*

Activities:

- ☐ **True love - page 111**
- ☐ **What fish? – page 113**
- ☐ **Future ideal – page 117**
- ☐ **Your client's shoes – page 121**

CHAPTER NINE

Bring your customers sunshine with your smile

Bring me sunshine with your smile…

in this world where we live there should be more happiness,

so much joy you can give to each brand new bright tomorrow…

bring me fun, bring me laughter, bring me love…

**Bring Me Sunshine
– Arthur Kent and Sylvia Dee**
(Signature tune for Morecambe & Wise)

The intention of this book is to inspire people to love their lives and businesses. A vital way to do that is to have fun while you're working at a job you enjoy. This chapter is all about enjoying being with your customers and transmitting love and fun.

You owe it to your clients to smile, be light and positive. Be a person they want to be around.

Another shopping example

Let's think supermarkets and shopping experiences. I just popped out to do some shopping and as I had bought fruit and veg there a few days ago, I thought about going back to the value European supermarket as opposed to my regular more expensive one. I could have done either, really easily. I decided to go to the pricier British one – why?

I just get the impression they like me in 'my' supermarket. They are always talking to me, giving me vouchers, little messages about how much I have saved. I know the other one is better value but it's dark and chaotic, and I can't find things easily and if I have more than three things to pack, the items fall on to the ground, because the cashier is in such a hurry and there is nowhere to pack the shopping. Would more space at the end of the till really cause a huge increase in prices?

Why do you buy from the people you buy from?

This is a very simple but powerful exercise. Answer this question:

Q. *Why* do I buy from the shops and companies that I buy from?

Write down a reason and then a brief sentence to justify it.

_____

_____

_____

_____

_____

_____

If you choose price, justify it. If we only cared about the price of things nobody would buy Jaguar, Mercedes, SuperDry or Hollister (for crying out loud!).

Was that a useful exercise? What did you learn about how you are as a customer?

I suspect you want a good, positive and considerate experience when you shop. With a smile if possible. So do your customers.

Look at your business from a different point of view. With each customer contact you create an experience, which could be positive, negative or so-so. It's time for you to manage proactively the creation of a positive experience with your client.

If you deliver your product or service with 'love', you will gain an edge in the market. Not only will you and your customers feel better, but it will positively affect your bottom line.

As a loving business owner your job is to make it as easy as possible for your clients to benefit from what you supply. In the last chapter you did some work to understand what challenges your customers, and potential customers, may need to overcome before they work with you, or your competitors.

> ### Wacky weeding
>
> Remember Lily, our example gardener? She has a long list of issues people may have with her gardening service. Here are a few again, to remind you:
>
> - *I need a gardener but I don't want chemicals all over the place because of my cat.*
> - *How do I find a gardener?*
> - *What if the gardener wants to work every week? I am not sure I need that.*
>
> Lily has come up with some ideas, perhaps wacky, in order to address these possible concerns:
>
> - *Measure the length of their grass and stick a card through the door saying 'Your grass is now five inches long, time for a short back and sides'.*
> - *Dress up in a pussycat costume and knock on doors explaining that this particular gardener is kind to pets.*
> - *Lily will communicate with clients however suits them best: Twitter, Facebook, text.*

- *Lily's contact details can be easily seen on her van.*
- *Lily has a PayPal account if they don't want to leave money under a doormat.*
- *Lily will negotiate flexible gardening contracts.*

Find solutions

OK here we go. Take a look at the list of challenges your clients face, that you brainstormed in the 'Walk in your client's shoes' previous chapter. Now is your chance to have some fun and come up with wild wacky ideas as to how you and your business might address those challenges.

_____

_____

_____

Does that make sense? If in doubt, find a potential customer or two and ask them! People love to be asked their opinion. They will give their time for free if they think you are considering their opinion.

In amongst your far-fetched ideas will be some practical solutions that you can apply.

Of course your competition will be offering tried and tested solutions too. Be aware of those, and implement the sensible ones, but what can you introduce that will make those feature solutions true to your Vision and Values, and define you as a more interesting fisherman?

Your products or services are gifts from you in order to solve your ideal client's challenges. Understanding that ensures you set your business up as client focused from the very beginning. Going through this form of market research is also a valuable way of checking that the product or service you are offering actually has a market.

FOWTW – Find Out What They Want – you have tackled. You have found out a little about what your customers want. You will learn more as your business develops.

The next step is to:

GAGI – *Go and Get It.*

Will the products and services you offer be what your clients have told you they want? If not, why not and what are you going to do? Your business will be more effective and profitable if you give your customers what they want, not what you think they should have.

And when you have it:

GITT – *Give It To Them.*

Keith does not mean give for free. People pay for what they value and value what they pay for. (A well-known marketing technique is to raise the price on a product.) You supply them with the product or service, as easily as possible.

Your next task is to ensure that *you* are clear on the *value* your product or service brings to your customer. If you are bringing sunshine into their lives you need to ensure they are aware of that, and they are also aware of the fact that no one else can bring them sunshine like you can, and they know how valuable that sunshine is for them.

Features, Advantages, Benefits, Results and Value

F A B – perfect for a superhero! For those of you that remember *Thunderbirds*.

Marketing is all about selling a product that doesn't come back (quality) to a customer that does (loyalty and value). So far you have considered your client's issues and concerns with your business, and you have a list of solutions you could introduce in order to address them; these are features of your product or service.

The FAB exercise is a way of ensuring that you always consider the benefits and results that your products or services provide, rather than the features. Same information, different point of view.

Here is an example – using an ordinary cup as the product.

Features are what a product has, what it is made up of, what it can do. So a cup contains liquid, has a handle, is made of a leak-proof material.

> As I write this I am thinking about a recent joke on BBC Radio advertising Best New Comedians; apologies, I can't remember the comic who said: "That coffee shop is promoting a refillable cup, well surely all cups are refillable, if they weren't they'd be tubes!" Tee hee!

Advantages: These are the positive implications of that feature. So the feature of a cup is that it has a sealed bottom, the *advantage* is that it can hold liquids and refills!

Benefits/Results: This is the KEY selling point. Benefit answers the question 'What's in it for me?' (Remember your solutions to your client's concerns?)

This is the value that the product feature has for the customer. If you can put the benefit in terms of results, that makes it really powerful. *Benefit result* of a cup is that you can carry your drink from one place to another without it pouring out all over your clothes.

This technique is particularly useful for products, but can be used for services too. Just set up a grid like the one below – the example this time shows the feature of a free refill – and work your way through.

Features	Advantages	Benefits/Results
Free refill of coffee when you buy one.	*You can have more coffee without paying for it.*	You can have as much coffee as you like without having to pay any more or go anywhere else. Save money and hassle.
Fair trade coffee.	*The coffee comes from producers that follow fair trade guidelines.*	Peace of mind that buying this coffee has not exploited anyone, so you feel better about yourself – priceless!

F A B

Now it's your turn. Look at your product or service's key features and think through the advantages and the benefits those features offer the customer.

Features	Advantages	Benefits/Results

Yes, it's an old ploy, but worth doing for each of your products and services. It offers another opportunity for you to think like your potential customer.

Transformation

The next technique is for those of you going into a service-focused business, e.g. coaching, hypnotherapy, consultancy etc.

This tool will help you define the transformation you offer. By transformation I mean the radical change, renewal or shift in how your clients live their lives as a result of working with you.

The headings are:

- ☐ **Life before:** *note the issue, worry or pain that the client has (see previous chapters).*
- ☐ **The change trigger:** *the therapy that you can implement that will change their lives, the solution that you offer to overcome their pain.*

- [ ] **How their life transforms:** *how your work can make their lives more amazing. The result of them implementing the change that you advise.*
- [ ] **Without transformation:** *what would the client's life be like without the change you offer them? The cost of them NOT taking this opportunity to transform.*

Example – this Jump Start book

Life before	The change trigger	How life transformed	Without transformation
Unsure about life as a solopreneur.	Read and worked through actions in this book.	Now more confident in Dream, Vision, Mission, knowing key steps to follow in order to set up a business that matches superpowers and life dreams.	Remaining in full-time employment, not knowing dream and gifts, feeling frustrated and unhappy.

Let's just do a quick sense check. We have been very client focused so far in this chapter and it's time to think about you and how you are feeling about this process.

Ask yourself – how do you feel when you deliver your product or service? Are you happy, excited, enthused? Are you keen to spread the news about how amazing your goodies are?

If you love your products then you will have the best chance of creating that love in your clients as well. If you love the experience of what you sell, then your clients will too.

Belief

Many of you will have heard, or even tried, the network marketing range Arbonne. I am an Arbonne consultant. I love the products. Their features are in tune with my way of thinking about natural ingredients, recyclable packaging and no animal testing. They also seem to be effective and feel good!

When I signed up as a consultant I thought network marketing was THE answer. I love the product, I loved the support from the team I had joined, I loved the thought of the rewards as I moved up the tree, particularly the Mercedes! I invested a lot of money, bought the kit as recommended, went into it full steam ahead, as I am wont to do when I start something new. I did really well, I got promoted to the next level within a few months, as predicted, but I did that through moving product, not by recruiting people, because I am a good salesperson and Arbonne is an excellent product.

The problem was that although I believed in the product, I never believed in my ability to build a team. Therefore I could sell product, but felt unable to recruit people, and that is a vital skill if you want

> to be successful at network marketing. I didn't believe in myself and my ability to transform my life, effectively, through being an Arbonne leader, so was unable to encourage others to believe, and the outcome was no team and no network marketing business.
>
> I didn't really commit to making it work and, as we have already discussed in a previous chapter, if you do not commit you will be found out.
>
> I have seen how people truly committed to Arbonne, and other network marketing companies, can make a success of it, real monthly income. So I commend you inspirational people, because that's who you are, and wish anybody who loves their network marketing product and team to go for it all guns blazing. You can succeed and help others too.

Be honest with yourself, are you committed to your business and to making it work? Are you happy? Does it fulfil you? Are you applying your gifts?

Give It To Them

If you have followed the steps to this point in the book you will now have the following material:

- *Vision, Mission, Values.*
- *An ideal structure for your working life: hours, place of work, client types etc.*

- *A high-level business plan, how your business will solve your clients' issues.*
- *Noted the features, benefits and results of your products and services, how your products will add value to your clients.*

We are now going to discuss the sales process, the Jump Start way, considering your approach and attitude rather than instructional to do list.

Having said that, have a quick look at your proposed sales process. How long is it from you initially contacting your customer to providing them with a way to buy into your product or service?

Simple lead to sale planner

The objective of this exercise is to plot the key steps your business follows in order to bring in your customers.

By the way, a 'lead to sale' plan, some call it a 'customer lifecycle', can be used as part of your business plan. As you build your business, record the numbers and percentages against each step as that provides useful information such as conversion rate of calls to clients.

Here is a typical example:

1. *Send letters.*
2. *Follow up contact.*
3. *Make appointment.*
4. *Have meeting.*
5. *Send proposal.*

6. *Follow up proposal – conversation presenting benefits and results of your offer.*
7. *Get deal – the sale.*
8. *Send invoice.*
9. *Get payment.*
10. *Start work.*

Your turn :

_____

_____

_____

_____

Now start reviewing your process by taking into consideration the following points:

- *How can you reduce the steps to the money? In the example above there are six steps between the contact with the client and the payment (step 4 to step 10). Can you tweak your process to get income sooner?*

- *Your clients and potential clients are so valuable. Remember your most valuable client last year? How much did you earn from them? Each of the people who visit your website, or who express an interest in you, could be that client. How are you treating them when they get on to your site? What have you got on your website that causes an action from the people that visit it? How are you capturing the information of those that are interested?*

- *Compare your sales process with the comments that your potential clients have made. What could you change that would surprise them?*
- *Do you have a contact system keeping track of your clients and potential clients?*

The Price Issue

How much are you going to charge? Many businesses make the mistake of undercharging for their goods or services.

One of the reasons given for not buying something, or selling something, is price. I have heard business people say: "Sue, we are in a credit crunch, no one has any money."

THAT IS JUST NOT TRUE! Remember the negative belief work? The western world has never been richer. We are shockingly wealthy, our lives are very abundant. In the western world we have been issued with first-class tickets. Do you know anyone that doesn't have a mobile phone or digital television? We give our children gadgets worth hundreds of pounds to take to school with them, from the age of six or seven!

In short, people will pay for what they value. People will pay for what gives them an amazing experience. People will pay for what they believe will transform their lives. **People will pay.**

The first thing you need to remember is not how much your product is worth but how much your product is worth to your client.

> **Deliver**
>
> I have just received two deliveries. The first was a headset from Amazon, not exciting but got to me very quickly, within two days. The second delivery was a beautifully presented bouquet of flowers with a little chocolate in the bow. Both deliveries delighted me because of the small touches showing people had put some thought into the experience.

Aim to under promise and over deliver when it comes to supply.

The tricky thing, of course, is that your clients get spoiled. If you set expectations you need to ensure that you live up to them. Put processes in place to ensure that you maintain your quality levels of contact and delivery. Have a tick sheet for key deliverables. Put key dates into a diary with reminders. Automate as much as possible.

Listen and learn from your clients and your experiences. Apply your learning and trust your instincts. Remember your Values and Mission and ensure that you keep congruent with that.

There have been a couple of interesting examples of companies doing that recently.

Cool talkin'

I was listening to the radio the other day. They were talking about the problem of young people being unhealthily overweight and the relationship to sugar and carbonated drinks and lack of exercise. The Chief Executive of Coca-Cola Europe was interviewed, live, as part of this subject. He was, of course, attacked for how Coca-Cola promotes sugary, carbonated drinks. He was calm and not defensive at all. He explained that his company supports initiatives which encourage children and young people to play and have fun, safely, outside. Coca-Cola also produces sugar-free drinks in order to offer 'healthier choices'.

He was actually asked how many Coca-Cola drinks he drank each day (full marks to the interviewer), and what he had drunk that day and, impressively, he said he drank one or two Cokes a day and had partaken of a Coke Zero that morning. (Apparently he occasionally has a full sugar Coke. Tut tut!)

The Coca-Cola guy had integrity and was congruent. No matter what you think of Coca-Cola (check out their Values by the way) their spokesman was walking their talk.

You must truly represent your business

Compare that with the banks. Oh, don't they keep shooting themselves in the foot, I almost feel sorry for them!

> Last year the Royal Bank of Scotland ran an advertising campaign that made me want to tear down their posters. I am one of their customers, through a subsidiary bank. They spent millions telling us how amazing their customer service was. Maybe there was one customer who got amazing service…
>
> Perhaps the millions spent on advertising might have been better spent supporting their customers through mortgages and loans for homes and small businesses.
>
> RBS banking systems have crashed twice in the last few months, preventing people from taking money out and paying bills. Once is forgivable, but twice? I am expecting a letter of apology. As yet there is no sign of one. Last year O2 crashed for a day, they sent a letter of apology and credited some rental, or something. The funny thing is that I did not even check that they had applied the credit; the main thing for me was the personal apology.
>
> The lesson? Learn to love and value the clients you already have before you go looking for new ones. Check with your clients that they are still feeling valued.

Don't treat your customers as you expect to be treated, treat them better than they expect. Love them. Appreciate them and say thank you. Thank you.

Next time you are going through an experience where you are being sold to, allow yourself to be a customer. You do not have to sign up. Don't run away. Don't try to control the experience, allow yourself to be served. How does it feel? Which companies look after you as you wish to be looked after? How do they do it? How can you introduce that into your service?

Oh, another tip. How do you treat the businesses that supply to you? Be seen to be a good, responsible and communicative customer and you will attract good customers.

> I am going away next week, a long haul flight! I have been meaning to treat myself to a large suitcase and last week I started looking around local big stores and the local discount outlet. A few years ago, when I was in Paris, I bought a suitcase because mine had disintegrated. Since then this French suitcase has done me proud. It's been bashed, thrown around trains, planes, boats, cars, everywhere, and I even seriously broke it and it accepted my repair and has been good since then. (Remember – market a product that doesn't come back...) I realised that I coveted a matching suitcase (... to a customer that does). So I went and found a luggage company through 'you know who' and have bought one.
>
> Amazon told me that the delivery date for my case will be four days after I fly out. I contacted the

seller and explained that I would have to cancel the order if that was the case – ooops, I mean situation. The seller, Gary, got back via email, stating delivery is actually today and that I would get a text advising me of that before 11am. I didn't get a text, so just emailed Gary, told him not to worry, I had not received a text but was happy if I got my suitcase this week. Gary has just phoned me. He has spoken to the delivery company (who told him they had sent me two texts – nope) and they will be delivering my new baby today, between 2.30 and 3.30pm. He was polite, friendly and had taken the time to call me to ensure I had personal contact. Gary addressed my pain and went a little bit out of his way to do so. He brought me sunshine with his smile.

Last word. After all we've covered in this chapter, this made me cry with laughter!

> *If I asked my customers what they wanted they would have said a faster horse*
>
> **– HENRY FORD**

Highlights

CHAPTER NINE

Bring you customers sunshine with your smile

- ✓ *Delivering your product and service with love will give you a market edge.*
- ✓ *If you love what you do, and your product, that enjoyment will transmit itself to your customers.*
- ✓ *Having fun, loving what you do, giving to others is living, not working.*
- ✓ *With each customer contact you are creating an experience, for you and your customer. What type of experience are you creating?*
- ✓ *Look at your business from your client's point of view.*
- ✓ *Ask them what difficulties they face and see what you can alter in your business to address those difficulties.*
- ✓ *Make it easy for them to buy from you, at all levels.*
- ✓ *FOWTW, GAGI, GITT.*
- ✓ *Be honest with yourself, are you happy doing this work? If not, do something about it.*

Activities:
- ☐ **Why do you buy from the people you buy from? - page 128**
- ☐ **Find solutions– page 131**
- ☐ **FAB - page 135**
- ☐ **Transformation - page 135**
- ☐ **Simple Lead to sale planner - page 139**

CHAPTER TEN
Broadcast your message and call in your clients (go fishing)

Doing business without advertising is like winking at a girl in the dark. You know what you are doing, but nobody else does

– STUART HENDERSON BRITT

Going fishing?

Have you have done the preparation you need to have done before you go out there and get your feet wet?

- ✓ *Positively decided that running a business is your sport?*
- ✓ *Have you a clear idea of how long you will spend working, e.g. hours per day, days per week, weeks per year etc.?*
- ✓ *Do you know what your talents are, what strengths to play to?*
- ✓ *Do you understand what you don't enjoy and what you need help with?*
- ✓ *You have written your Vision, Mission and Values.*
- ✓ *You have decluttered your path of limiting beliefs and useless wellies.*

✓ *You know who your clients are, what they like to eat, where they like to swim.*

✓ *You have a better idea as to how to market your business.*

If you have done all that then you are ready. And pat yourself on the back because if you *have* done all that work then you are already much better prepared than the majority of businesses at start-up. You have a Jump Start!

And please remember, you wouldn't go fishing without a licence, appropriate clothing – well, decent footwear at least – and probably an experienced fisherman, for the first couple of times.

In other words, there is no need to buy your business cards, build your web page or join networking groups until you are clear about why you are going to do what you are going to do, how you are going to do it, who for and how much you are going to charge. Kipling's six honest men.

Right, let's go fishing. This chapter is about bait and how often to cast your line. This is not about casting a huge net and making the most of what you pick up, throwing away the tiddlers and the tough big ones. No, this is about transmission on the right frequency to the right people base, catching the right fish, using the right bait. Environmentally friendly fishing.

The message that you will transmit will be like the perfect wiggly worm on a hook. It will be attractive, informative and specific – perfect bait for the tasty fishes.

Here are some ways of packaging your business bait.

Message Method 1 – Tell a story

Tell a story. Stories work. Look at the Bible. The Bible is the original self-help manual and promotional brochure. In the Old Testament you find the 10 Commandments – the brief to do list, the key rules, the 10 easy steps to Heaven. The rest of the Bible is full of stories that explain how different people put those rules into action. It also explains the horrors that befall those who defy the rules. The iconic and most successful personal development book, we have been copying the Bible's structure ever since!

Stories have been told since humans could communicate. The best stories involve all five senses and leave you with a very clear picture about what is going on. The other amazing fact about stories is that the human brain cannot resist them. As soon as someone starts telling a story we tune in and listen. We have been learning by listening to stories since we were children; reading books, watching TV and movies, telling jokes, watching advertisements.

Think about your ideal client scenario, you may already have a real client who has been through this scenario (great, get a testimonial, a later method).

How to structure the story...

Once upon a time there was a xxx and here you put in your (potential) client with a problem, describe the problem in detail and how it is making your client suffer, be unhappy and face difficulties. Describe the problem in detail, affecting as many senses as possible. The problem becomes the dragon, witch, baddy, fatal flaw. The problem you describe is one of the problems you solve, of course. Enter the knight(ess) in shining armour and what do you do? You will probably have seven easy steps, A.B.C. or 10 Commandments in order to slay the monster. Remember the monster is actually the pain the client is feeling, not the situation they are in.

Story example

I remember a Big Al (network marketing guru) story which goes a little bit like this.

Note: the crucial word here is remember. I didn't need to look this story up, or listen again to Big Al, I remembered the story. I am a person who can't remember jokes, except two very visual silly jokes, so this must be a very powerful technique.

'A friend of mine, Bob, went into work one day and, as he was sitting at his desk, he felt a tap on his shoulder, he looked up and there was his boss looming over him. "Do you want the good news or the bad news first?" asked his boss. Bob asked for the bad news first. "I am letting you go," said his boss, "the Chinese have taken most of our business and we are reducing our staff costs." Bob felt sick, he had just booked a holiday and was wondering how he was going to tell his wife and children that they were not going to see the sunshine that year because their holiday would need to be cancelled. He thought of his mortgage, visualised his red bank statement, saw his retirement party disappearing. He could feel his stomach churn and the cold sweat break out on his forehead. "What is the good news?" asked Bob hopefully. "You have the rest of the day off!" replied his boss.

Bob was desperate. "What can I do? There must be something?" "Well," said his boss hesitantly, "there is a way. If you work an extra hour every evening, and a couple of hours at the weekend, for no pay, after three years you will be able to retire with a full pension and never have to worry about money again." So Bob started to do this. He worked an hour after work until 6.30pm every day. After a few months his wife started to complain, he was late for tea and it disrupted her evenings. He explained that he would only be a little late, would cook sometimes and that, just imagine, in only three years they would both be able to stop work.

The summer came and Bob was invited to a barbecue, scrummy sausages, but he explained that he would be late because he was working. His friends teased him for working at the weekend. Bob was frustrated but was determined to show that he had earned his retirement. He kept at it. And, after two and a half years, Bob went into work and tapped his boss on his shoulder. "Do you want the good news or the bad news?" You can guess the rest.

> Sadly most companies do not offer this kind of facility but if you join a network marketing company you too could be tapping your boss on his shoulder and retiring on a wonderful, safe, bountiful income after only three years. And you will never have to work again.'

OK it's cheesy, but I reckon there's a little voice inside of you going 'Hmm, network marketing eh?'

It's important that your story is realistic and believable.

This story could very well be true; there are a lot of people who have made a great deal of money at network marketing, the money keeps coming in even after you stop 'working'.

Anyhow – that's not the point, the point is to have a story.

Your story will clearly describe how your products or services help your suffering potential clients transform their lives so they can handle the dragon, understand how to work around the monster or chase away the baddy, and then feel beautiful, popular and wealthy, living happily ever after.

Write your story

_____

_____

_____

Message Method 2 – Elevator pitch

Named for the theory that you have the length of an elevator ride to tell someone what you do in an exciting way, so that they ask you more questions when the doors open.

Most networking events give you at least a minute to make your pitch. Big Al had a couple of ideas as to how to use that minute. I quite like this one:

Truth, truth then teaser.

Network Marketing example: Many young people are unemployed (truth). Many young people like new cars (truth). Some young people are self-employed working for a company that will give them a new Mercedes, for free, if they keep at it.

Jump Start book example: Many people who are made redundant become self-employed. For many of them the first thing they invest in is business cards yet their business fails. Many entrepreneurs I know are incredibly successful and do not have business cards. Jump Start shows you how to start a successful business, with or without business cards.

Write a teasing elevator pitch

_____

_____

_____

Message Method 3 – Testimonials

The 'sweet spot' time to get testimonials is just when you have supplied your customer with the product or service and they are happy. Don't wait until that exultation dies away.

If your customer does not know how to give you a testimonial, tell them what to say and send them a link so they can post it easily. Have an automatic process, think about Sky or O2. Thwack, within half a day of calling their technical help desk the texts come in and ask for feedback. That feedback goes towards the stats they provide to the City, shareholders and other customers.

Remember '90% of customers who expressed a preference said their cats preferred Whiskas'? That statement is influential on several levels. People like to feel that they are in with the in-crowd, and also that there is proven success. If possible, and appropriate, include numerical information within your testimonial.

For example: 'Working with Sue not only gave me a good insight into my strengths, but since becoming more confident about how to serve my clients better my net profit has increased by 30%.'

Testimonial

Write your ideal client's perfect testimonial for you.

_____

_____

_____

Message Method 4 – Have a quick answer to "And what do you do?"

My answer:

> *"I show people how to have fun,
> loving what they do for people they love, and
> have a successful business."*

Please don't stress over this, it's supposed to be fun. Experiment! Have a catch phrase or a little rhyme.

Answer "And what do you do?"

_____

_____

_____

> A few months ago my car was blocked in at my accountant's car park when I started chatting to a Wealth Management chap who knew whose car had blocked me.
>
> He asked me what I did, I said: "Err…" He laughed and said: "You must be a business consultant then!" I laughed but felt mightily embarrassed. An invaluable lesson. Know what you do.

How to broadcast your message

How do you tell people about your business? With a smile, enthusiasm and certainty, that's more or less it.

Remember you don't tell everybody everything, but you can tell people an answer to the 'What do you do?' question.

Just recently I have been telling people what I do with a little too much enthusiasm; I can see their eyes widening. I am learning to be less effusive, but at least it's positive. Better to be known as the enthusiastic business coach than the bored and boring one.

As we discussed earlier in the book, remember that once you start telling people about your business, you represent your business. Therefore think about how you remain congruent with your Mission and Values. When you are out and about, you are the image of your company.

Bear in mind how you look. Be clean and shiny and smart, in order to seem attractive to your client but true to who you are. I know that many of you will do jobs that are mucky or sweaty; perhaps you are a personal trainer, or a farmer, or a decorator. That does not prevent you from being shaved or smartly hairy, and wearing a clean outfit, maybe with a logo, when you meet people. Always, always, always wear a smile. A happy, positive one too. And do not mumble. Head up, shoulders back, be proud. Remember you like being you and you are a superhero.

I always remember one of my coaches saying that she walks into a room assuming that people will love her. Not just *like* her, *love* her. You know that is difficult to do, but no more difficult than walking into a room full of strangers and assuming people will not like you. If you love yourself, why wouldn't others love you? Change the voices in your head. Remember that you are an amazing person and that you are brilliant at being you. Who would you rather buy from and work with? A happy, confident smiling person or a grump? Make a decision and commit, and honestly, which you is going to be more fun?

Let everyone know what you do in a way that interests your clients and informs all. Think about the fishing analogy. There are other fish in the river, but you just want your ideal type. The wording of the message needs to hook the right people. So you ensure that it is clear who you will work with, and who you will not.

My quick answer to what I do is: "I show people that they can have fun, loving what they do for people they love and have a successful business." Let's dissect that statement. What words are my bait? What fish am I attracting?

I am aiming at:

- ✓ *People thinking about their own business.*
- ✓ *Unhappy business people who like to have fun, because I can transform them into happy business people having fun.*
- ✓ *People who do not have a successful business.*

So I am not aiming at at-home parents or the retired, I am not aiming at job-seekers or the employed, and I am not aiming at people who are already having fun running a successful business – although they may just get hooked in because they can never have enough fun.

Let's do a similar statement for Lily, our gardener.

What do we know about her? That she can make your garden look beautiful, without hurting the local wildlife and pets and she is easy to communicate with.

Q: "What do you do, Lily?"

A: "If you love your pets and nature, want a beautiful garden but never have time to think about it let alone weed it, then I am the gardener for you. Obedient, contactable and trainable – just whistle and I am there."

OK, the statement needs work but what does it do? It tells everybody that Lily is a gardener. She is not a gardener for everybody, just for those who love nature and pets. If you are busy and aspire to a beautiful garden, then she will hook you too. She is easy to work with. And has a sense of humour. So no, Lily will not appeal to everyone, but that is not the point. She needs only to appeal to the people that want a trustworthy, easy, friendly, nature-loving gardener.

This is the value of bait, and the reason why it is so important to understand who your ideal client is, and who your ideal client is not. You cannot start marketing until you have this clearly in your head. It's the Marmite factor. Some people will love your hook and others hate it. That is OK; not only is it OK, it is great! You become cool. You become niche. You become specialist. The more specific the bait, the clearer your niche, the more successful your broadcast will be.

Remember you are a superhero with specific superpowers. You can only use your superpowers to save and help the people who **understand they need your particular skills and value them**. No point in trying to help anyone else. It saves pain, misunderstanding and hassle. So broadcast clearly to the relevant people. And don't take offence or take it personally if the irrelevant people aren't hooked. Some Will, Some Won't, So What, Move On. SWSWSW!

Which channels to use?

We go back to the importance of understanding who your client is. There is no point in broadcasting how amazing you are on Facebook if your ideal client does not value or use Facebook. Believe it or not, there are still many people, with lots of disposable income, who do not use Facebook.

It may be valuable to discuss the different communication 'channels' (communication mediums) that you could use to broadcast your message. Here are a few suggestions that are of little or no cost, also known as 'below the line'. Please accept a health warning: these are just my thoughts. I will not have taken everything into consideration – there is, after all, so much to consider!

Channel	+	-
Voice: 1 to 1 *Telephone call*	*Live one-to-one communication is very powerful and there is no harm in calling people you know and telling them what you are doing. Have a reason.* *If calling people you don't know, do as follow-up to an email or letter. Or call following an accepted pre-agreement. For example, a warranty has run out or annual check required, or you have a new service relevant for them.* *Always good opportunities. Call people you have met, or that have been recommended. Be smiley, positive and clear on your reason for calling. Ask for permission to call again.* *A phone call is also great because you get the benefit of powerful personal contact through a very low-cost medium.*	Avoid cold calling unless you are 100% sure of your client type and message. Also very difficult to verify lists so can be time costly. Unless one of your superpowers is phone conversation, bear in mind it is a skill which can be learned but takes time and confidence to learn. Only do it if you enjoy it. It's time consuming, frustrating but very powerful to win people over more strongly, and to get direct response.

Channel	+	-
Voice: 1 to many Webinar/ teleconference	An opportunity for you to broadcast your message to people who have expressed an interest in learning more about you and your product or service. For those of you who don't know, it's a virtual seminar. You do it live or pre-record, I recommend live. You can use PowerPoint or similar software should you choose, or just talk over a 'blank' screen. Use webinars to give people an experience of your training, coaching, business for little cost, or free, and gain useful customer contact information.	You will need webinar software and kit; there are several low-cost versions. Consider where you will promote your webinar: LinkedIn, Facebook and your email list. Let as many people know as possible. If you don't get many people listening live, that's OK, you can use the webinar as a resource on your website or YouTube.
Voice: 1 to many Radio	Contact your local radio station. Let them know you are available as an 'expert' for your specialist subject. This will get you known as an authority and raise awareness of your business name. Useful to write a brief email with reasons why you are a good person for this particular station to talk to.	There are techniques to help you get noticed, I recommend coaching with someone successful at this. DO NOT use radio opportunities to blatantly advertise on air.

Channel	+	-
Face to Face Networking	*Can be really useful in two ways: if your ideal client goes to this type of network group, or if it's a networking group that focuses on providing leads and is successful for your type of business. If you don't know, ask other successful people in your business if they network and which ones they have found useful. As most networking groups focus on taking time to get to know who you are and what you do, it can be valuable experience and a perfect time to practise your elevator speech.*	It can be time-consuming and expensive. Be prepared to investigate different groups to find the ones that suit you. You are likely to make some good contacts and acquaintances. Remember your objectives and be pragmatic.
Face to face 1:1 Interactive	*Nothing better. Have meetings with your potential clients but ensure there is a purpose behind it and not just an opportunity to chat. This is a time to listen to them, find out what is good and what is not working. Use these meetings as opportunities to see if you have a product or service that can serve them. This is the most powerful way to broadcast your message.*	Remember when meeting new people, even in a social setting, if you are there in your business capacity, be responsible and congruent. Each ideal client contact is precious, take their details, ask for permission to contact them. Treat their business card with respect.

Channel	+	-
Visual Speaking live 1: many 1: interactive	Get as many gigs as you can where your client type is likely to be. Good opportunity to broadcast your message. Volunteer, adding 'speaker' to your credits helps with your authority. Also great time to get information and feedback about your market.	Get some training, unless you are a confident and experienced speaker. Have an objective for all talks. Plan and structure it.
Visual TV	With lots more local stations and online TV stations popping up this can be a great fun, if scary, opportunity to literally broadcast.	Would get coaching from specialist; in summary be prepared and be early. And remember, like radio, using free airtime to advertise yourself is the kiss of death for future appearances.
Visual Video 1: many	It will be worth getting a video of you talking about your product or service and posting it on your website, YouTube and anywhere else you think it may be useful. Marketing is all about building up a relationship with your clients, and potential clients will expect to see photos of you at least.	Ensure the video is of good quality, think passport photos. If you post an awful video anywhere, it will turn up in the most unexpected places!

Channel	+	-
Virtual 1: many YouTube	*YouTube is now used as much as Facebook to gather information about people, possibly more so for businesses. Take advantage of that and consider posting some informative videos about you and what you do. If you would like to guide, teach and help people, use this channel to offer 'how to' guides, gather a following. Interlink with blogs and emails.*	Do your best to keep control of what is posted on YouTube. Check regularly what is on the web about you to ensure that the public material is congruent and supportive of your business.
Social Media: Facebook 1: many 1: interactive	*Facebook can be invaluable as part of your broadcasting plan. It allows you to communicate with people who are interested in you. You can also manage people effectively by building groups. Business page, or a fan page, can also be useful. You can track how your 'tribe' grows as Facebook provides useful statistics.* *Facebook is a giant social sandpit – for the very confident!*	I recommend working with a social media expert, if you are not one, in order to think through and understand how best to harness the power of Facebook. And remember, if your ideal clients don't use it, there is less point in promoting your business directly on it. Do tell your friends what you do though and direct interested people to where they can find more information.

CHAPTER TEN - Broadcast your message and call in your clients (go fishing)

Channel	+	-
Twitter **1: many** **1: interactive**	Twitter is a very good way to keep a track of issues that may affect your product or service type. It is also a good way to see what your competitors are up to. It is brilliant for keeping you up-to-date with key trends and ensuring you are seen to be in with the in-crowd. Twitter is also ideal for building up your 'tribe' and encouraging them to visit your web page.	**Twitter is addictive, but fun. If your client type uses it then be seen there.** **Manage your time. Be very careful what you post. What's tweeted cannot be untweeted.**
LinkedIn **1: many**	Historically, the people on LinkedIn tend to have been corporate professionals and employees. However LinkedIn has adapted and grown and is now used by all types of business people. It is a network to do business on, very CV and commercial achievement based. If your enterprise is business-to-business then it is likely your potential clients are on LinkedIn, making it the place for you. There are many special interest groups supporting more specific networking within LinkedIn. Take a look, or create your own.	**Rule Number One: only invite people that you have met, or know, to join you on Linked In. If possible send them a personalised invitation. Remember this is a business focused network, not Facebook. If new to LinkedIn, have a nose around and see how others are using the network and the tone of their posts.**

Channel	+	-
Others	There are other internet-based social networks, many of them are specialist. Know your clients and find out where they look for information about your products.	
Written: Newspapers	Another channel which raises awareness of you as an authority on a particular topic. Use local newspapers to promote work you are doing in the community, or if you have a people interest story. Ask yourself: "If it wasn't my business would I still be interested?" If the answer is no, rewrite or don't send. Think about two or three key messages that you want to transmit. Write a very brief press release and remember to answer the How, What, Why, Where, When, Who questions. Put your contact details on the email so you can be contacted for further information. Include photos.	Get a contact name first and call them and ask if they are the right people for the information. Have the email release ready to send as soon as you have finished the call. Newspapers and online papers want a story, something newsy, interesting, current. They will cut the whole article if it looks or reads like an advert, known as 'puff'.

Channel	+	-
Magazines	What does your ideal client read? Trade magazines? Local freebies? Consider writing an article. Contact the editor and read the magazine to get an understanding of the style of the articles.	Keep the article light, chatty and informative. Use quotes from key people. Get photographs. Remember, write it in a way that you would enjoy reading it.
Online articles Blogs	A great opportunity to build your writing muscles. Your blog is likely to be found if someone does a search for you and therefore you can write information and articles more wordy than tweets or Facebook posts for people who want to learn more about you.	

Highlights

CHAPTER TEN

Broadcast your message and call in your clients (go fishing)

- ✓ *They're not going to know if you don't tell them – so tell them.*
- ✓ *Make the message specific to your ideal client – think fishing: what will entice them?*
- ✓ *If your message is specific enough others will hear what you do, but your ideal clients will listen and remember and search you out.*
- ✓ *Think of a story to tell that shows how you solved a customer's problem.*
- ✓ *Have a few answers to the 'What do you do?' question. All fun and specific.*
- ✓ *Get testimonials as soon as you have delivered the product or service. That's when your client is most positive.*
- ✓ *Remember to present yourself in a way that is attractive to your potential clients.*
- ✓ *Where does your client look for information? Be there.*
- ✓ *Build experience broadcasting your message on 'below the line' channels.*

Activities:

- ☐ **Storytelling - page 154**
- ☐ **Elevator pitch – page 155**
- ☐ **Testimonial – page 156**
- ☐ **Answer "What do you do?" – page 157**

CHAPTER ELEVEN
Don't be afraid to make mistakes

Ten chapters of this little book have been about preparation. Ensuring that you have a clear idea about who you are, your special talents, the things you like doing and what you want to do. You now have a wonderful dream for your life and a clear Vision for your business. You know who your clients are and what to say to them. You have looked at your wardrobe, office space, life and you are a lean prepared machine. We haven't been specific about your product or service, but to be honest this preparation is vital no matter what business you are in.

Now it is time to put it all into action. Go out and make mistakes.

Let's tackle a few beliefs that you may have about action. I am going to make a list of the phrases I have heard – and suggest slight modifications.

- ✓ *'If you're going to do it, do it right.' Rubbish. If you're going to do it, know why and do it.*
- ✓ *'If at first you don't succeed, try, try again.' Rubbish. If at first you don't succeed, try something else.*
- ✓ *'Fail to prepare, prepare to fail.' Hmmm. Over prepare and nothing happens.*

Some other things I would like you to bear in mind before you go and take action.

If at first you don't succeed:

- ✓ *Tell yourself how amazing, brave and great you were for trying it out.*
- ✓ *Think about what you learned – what went wrong, what went well, what you will change for next time.*
- ✓ *Adjust, change, learn.*
- ✓ *Book a date for the next experiment.*

Be happy to make mistakes, everybody does, but learn from them and try not to make exactly the same mistake twice. If you do make the same mistake twice then perhaps you need help in order to learn other ways of doing things, and that's OK too. Remember, the definition of insanity is doing the same thing over and over and expecting a different result. An objective, experienced eye can often see what you cannot and offer advice or training so that you can surmount the obstacle and move on.

I have worked with coaches over the last couple of years and without their support I would still be making the same mistakes.

Attract your luck

Perhaps you believe in the commonly held view of the Law of Attraction? You may have a clear idea about how you want your life to be, and you may be visualising the money coming in, but remember the joke about the guy who imagined himself winning the Lottery. He had read The Secret (admittedly only halfway through) and was imagining the cheque coming through the door. All that lovely money in his account. He did this every night for a week until the Lottery draw, and he didn't win. OK, he thought, I just need to imagine more clearly. He thought about piles of gold on his bed, rolling around and feeling those gold sovereigns running through his fingers. The next Lottery draw passed and he didn't win. He got a bit grumpy then, but thought that he still wasn't imagining hard enough. He carried around his tenner in his wallet and imagined it multiplying until all the tenners were too much to carry and they fluttered around him like confetti while he rushed around picking them up in big sacks. That week he did not win either. And he called out: "I am doing everything I am supposed to, I am imagining really hard, writing all my lists and my journal, saying my money aspirations, why aren't I winning the Lottery?" And the clouds parted and a deep booming voice called: "You have to buy a bloody Lottery ticket first!"

Time to buy the ticket folks. Time to get in the queue.

Take imperfect action, it's better to do something based on your good ideas and intuition than no action at all. Ah – but you are not sure what to do, are you?

Get your motor running

When I worked at Sky I went to a conference hosted by a Scottish chap, Jack Black, who was a very successful life coach speaker in the 1990s/2000s.

At one point he was talking about moving towards your dreams. This resonated with dreamless me and I put my hand up to ask a question; the auditorium was full of hundreds of people and yet he saw me! I said I didn't know how to dream, let alone have a dream, so how could I move?

He asked me to imagine a car in the middle of a car park and that I was in the driving seat. It could be that I didn't know where I wanted to go, but I did know that I didn't want to stay in that car park? "Yes." He told me to start the engine and drive out of the car park, because once the engine was on and the car was moving it would be so much easier for me to go somewhere. But if I stayed sitting in the car, frightened to turn on the engine because I was too overwhelmed by the thought that I didn't know what to dream, let alone that I could have dreams that I could make come true, nothing would ever change. I would never move, I would remain stuck. So Jack suggested I start the car, warm the engine and drive around the car park looking for the way out. It's so much easier to get on the open road towards your dreams if your car is moving!

It is easy to be so overwhelmed by the life-changing stuff, even after all your preparation, that you never cast off from the safe harbour of 'do as you have always done'. You never make that jump. What can make it even more painful is that you have glimpsed the shimmer of opportunity and fulfilment on the horizon; perhaps it would have been better had you never known there was another way, a happier place?

We have all been there. The big stuff is scary, it has to be. So build up your courage. Practise small actions like starting a sport, losing a bit of weight, writing a gratitude diary. Set a small objective, like walk three times a week, or lose 1lb a week. Plan your time, measure your progress, reward your success. That's how you build up confidence, focus and stamina and *then* you are ready to go for the big stuff like starting your own business!

Business Plan

Here is a structure for a very simple plan of action which could be done on a couple of sides of paper. This will provide you with the key ingredients of a business plan, a to do list giving you a jump-start towards your dream business.

- ✓ ***Understand your starting point. Where are you now?***
    - *You could do a SWOT analysis: list your Strengths, your Weaknesses, Opportunities for your business, Threats to your business (competitors, finances, time, knowledge).*

- *Do some measures, e.g.:*
  - *Current financial state of business, profit, cash flow, turnover.*
  - *How many clients?*
- *Subjective measures, e.g.:*
  - *How happy are you? Health?*
  - *What do your clients say?*

✓ Where would you like to be?

- *Your Dreams, Vision, Mission (tick).*
- *SMART objectives:*
  - *Specific*
  - *Measurable*
  - *Achievable*
  - *Realistic*
  - *Time based – one year, three years, five years*
- *Financial measures.*
- *Structure of the business, your time in it, how you will make money.*
- *How you would like to feel: happy, healthy etc. What do you do to feel that way?*

✓ How are you going to do it?

- *You know where you want to be in one year or three years – what do you need to do each month in order to achieve that?*
- *Write a to do list, or two or three – focus on the actions that will bring in the money.*
- *Make a note of key measures that you are going to keep an eye on in order to track your progress.*

- *Chunk your plan into mini plans:*
  - *- Financial plan*
  - *- Customer Communication plan*
  - *- The Spring plan*
  - *- The Summer plan*

✓ **Result**
- *Value.*
- *Lessons learned.*
- *What worked and why?*

Procrastination

Let's talk a little bit about procrastination – also known in the States as yak shaving.

'Yak Shaving is an activity that you do that appears important when you are consciously or unconsciously procrastinating about a larger problem.'

It's incredible how important organising my candles becomes when I am trying to finish this book!

I was going to tell you about two opposing theories with the intention of preventing you beating yourself into a pulp for not doing something, instead of doing it. And then I realised that the two theories are the same thing.

Accept that you will procrastinate. Overcoming the need to procrastinate is a skill, just like everything else.

Procrastination is a sign that you are not quite ready to do something and that you need to ask yourself what additional oomph you need in order to do it. Perhaps your energy is just not vibrating at the correct level for you to do your thing, and you may as well wait until you feel ready; and then, when you do feel ready, it will all fall into place and amazing things will happen. The point is that if your mind is not 'tuned in' then you will not create effectively when you sit yourself down to do something.

> **Anything but…**
>
> I was a bit like that yesterday; I wanted so much to work on the book and get some words in, but things kept happening to me, or I did irrelevant things. I updated the programme on my phone, first time for 14 months at least. No wonder it took several hours. Then I had a kerfuffle with a virus on my email and loads of people contacting me going 'what's this?' Then I decided to change details on my flight, couldn't get through on the phone so wandered into Facebook – that was a stupid mistake. I hadn't been there for months either. Oh – is that what she's doing now?!
>
> I am more on track today and writing better because of it.

I love the argument that procrastination is down to 'low vibrations', but think it's a little too gentle on us. Another coach is more pragmatic and states that procrastination is to do with fear. (Argh, I wish my cat would go away, she keeps insisting on being stroked!)

CHAPTER ELEVEN - Don't be afraid to make mistakes

Fear is caused by three different things, and if we recognise that we put off doing things because we are frightened, we can ask ourselves what we are frightened of and tackle that.

- *We are frightened because something is fuzzy. Because we are unclear as to what we need to do. The answer? Understand what we don't understand and ask for help, or do what we do know. Or do it in a way that we do understand. Look for clarity.*

- *We feel fear because the task seems to be too big. We are never going to be able to call 100 customers or write a book. The answer? Well, as you all know, the way to eat an elephant is little piece by little piece. My mind went wandering there, sifting through elephant jokes. All I could remember is the one about the elephant who paints his toenails red so that he can be found if he falls upside-down into a bowl of custard. Anyway I digress – you think? Chunk up your action into little pieces that you can do. Work out a timescale and do it a little at a time.*

- *And of course we feel fear because we believe we are unable to do something. Well, as your mum used to say, there's no such thing as can't! If it's an action you have agreed to do, you must have been able to do it otherwise it wouldn't be with you to do. You can probably do it if you set your mind to it and follow action plan for fuzzy or too big!*

> *A life spent making mistakes is not only more honourable, but more useful, than a life spent doing nothing.*
>
> **GEORGE BERNARD SHAW**
> **IRISH DRAMATIST AND SOCIALIST (1856 - 1950)**

It's time to move your behind.

Stuart's story

Let me tell you about Stuart. Stuart is amazing. But of course you all are!

Stuart is Glaswegian born and bred. He lives by the guidelines of the Law of Attraction. He studied with Jack Black too. Ten years or so ago, Stuart lost everything. His home, his marriage, his children went to live with his ex-wife and he was thousands of pounds in debt. He read The Secret and other books, and started to sort his life out. He saved money. And built his business. He worked hard and implemented the tools that good self-help books gave him.

He told me a great one that I have adopted. If he thinks a negative thought he makes an action with his hand to pull the imagined thought out of his head and throw it out of the window. He actually opens the window to do it! Wonderful.

Stuart runs a business that he is determined to grow, and cannot understand one thing. He doesn't understand why his team will not set objectives, targets or even a simple to do list for each day, week or month.

Stuart has a point. No matter what you believe in – the Law of Attraction, Abraham-Hicks or practical business advice – that which you focus on changes. You need to know what you want. And then you need to ask for it and work towards it, and help it happen. Hence the requirement for a to do list.

Stuart told me to put this in the book, and it is another one of his tips that I use. We are in the contacting people business. Write down the names of 20 people that you would like to do business with that month, with their phone numbers. You don't need to write down more than 20, you could write down only 10, five or two. If they do business with you, great, that's a big tick. If they don't do business with you that month but they will the next month, follow them on, cross out the ones who aren't interested. It is your list of heartthrobs! Thank you, Stuart.

And why don't the team write down their objectives? See above!

Have a to do list, and prioritise the to dos that use your gifts to bring in the income. Do the hardest things first.

And remember to review what you do and learn from your mistakes.

Well done and thank you.

JumpStart *The* Start Up Book *for* your Dream Business

CHAPTER ELEVEN
Don't be afraid to make mistakes

- ✓ *If at first you don't succeed – pat yourself on the back and tell yourself you did well for trying.*
- ✓ *Think about what you have learned from your action.*
- ✓ *Assess if you want to do that again – pros and cons.*
- ✓ *Have a plan – where are you now? Where are you going? What do you need to do and when in order to get there? And then review it.*
- ✓ *Experiment.*
- ✓ *Watch what others do – would that work for you, how can you improve it?*
- ✓ *Procrastination.*
- ✓ *Fear.*
- ✓ *Action.*

Activities:
- ☐ **Business Plan**
   - page 175

I've come to believe that each of us has a personal calling that's as unique as a fingerprint – and that the best way to succeed is to discover what you love and then find a way to offer it to others in the form of service, working hard, and also allowing the energy of the universe to lead you.

OPRAH WINFREY,
O MAGAZINE, SEPTEMBER 2002
US ACTRESS AND TELEVISION TALK SHOW HOST (1954 -)

Finally

This book aimed to advise you on the key steps you need to follow in order to have a great business having fun, loving what you do, attracting amazing clients and making money.

It was written for you.

Please use the book in whatever way brings you enjoyment and fun. And let me know. **www.suevizard.com**

Everything is working out for you. You are in the right place and you know the right things and you are exactly right, just as you are. And so is everyone else. Please love yourself more today than you did yesterday, and more tomorrow than you do today. Please appreciate others for the amazing people that they are too, and remember the only person you can control is yourself.

And, of course, I leave you with two inspirational song lyrics:

Flanagan and Allan

Are you havin' any fun? What you getting out of livin'?
What good is what you got
If you're not
Havin' any fun?

And

Dolly Parton – Better get to Livin'

I said you better get to livin', givin',
Be willing and forgivin',
Cause all the healing has to start with you.
You better stop whining, pining,
Get your dreams in line
And then just shine, design, refine
Until they come true
And you better get to livin'.

I wish you every success and lots of love and fun.

Sue

References and people to help you out of the car park

Judymay Murphy – **www.judymaymurphy.tv**

Lucie Bradbury – **www.DamselsInSuccess.co.uk**

Katharine Dever – **www.katharinedever.com**

Gay Hendricks – *The Big Leap* **www.hendricks.com**

Mindy Gibbins Klein – **www.bookmidwife.com**

Dan Bradbury – **www.danbradbury.com**

Abraham-Hicks – **www.abraham-hicks.com**

Pachamama Institute – **www.pachamama.org**

Seth Godin – **www.sethgodin.com**

Keith J Cunningham - **www.keystothevault.com**

Tom 'Big Al' Shreiter – **www.fortunenow.com**

Marianne Williamson – **www.marianne.com**

Jonathan Smith – **www.riverparkifa.com**

Jane Nelson – **www.janenelsoninteriors.com**

Rose O'Connor – **www.edenconsultancygroup.co.uk**

Ruth Mckay – **www.souniq.co.uk**

About the author

Sue Vizard is a woman on a mission. Having worked for large corporations like BT and Sky, Sue decided it was time to follow her calling and make the leap into self- employment. She made a commitment to living from her passions and as a result has travelled to far-flung destinations discovering life enhancing techniques, written her first book and discovered a renewed love and faith in life, her relationships and herself. She now shares her teachings with others who desire to create a life they truly love with her blog, books, talks, events and retreats.

You can get her life-changing and unique business Start-up Guide here:

www.suevizard.com

Testimonials

"Sue Vizard is a voice of the times- she is the embodiment of a fresh, optimistic new paradigm that says 'You Are Enough' and cheerleads you all the way to your biggest dreams. I love this book and I love what it will inspire in you- A resounding YES to your True Self. It's such a pleasure to read this book, Sue's enthusiasm is infectious- and will encourage you to inspired and effortless action and flow!'"

Katharine Dever,
Intuitive Business Mentor

"Sue is an inspiration. You cannot help but be enthused by her love of life and desire to help others achieve their full potential. This book shares the very essence of her experience, and is a must for anyone who needs help to get 'unstuck' in business."

Liz Melville
Social media consultant and mumpreneur

" It is a vivid road map confirming Sue knows what she is talking about and can empathise with the plight of the reader...brilliant"

Peter Marshall,
Partner, First Commercial Group

"Clear, concise advice how to deal with ambiguity in life."

Grace McNabola,
Entrepreneur

"I love this book! Part of what makes it such a joy to read is Sue's sharing of her own experiences. She really understands. You can't help but feel motivated and inspired!"

Catriona Staddon,
Director, Hyndberry

"A quote I always like is William Wallace in movie Braveheart when he is addressing the Scottish 'army' - when he asks them about surrendering then lying dying in their beds many years from now, would they be willing to trade all their days from then until now for one chance, just one chance, to go back and take their freedom. I liken that to somebody who is employed and fearful about embarking upon leaving to start their own business.

Congratulations. Sue has kept it conversational whilst still stirring thought."

Jonathan Smith,
Independent Financial Adviser